...which I would take ...
...asuming given them to ...
...ng to hear that you have ...
...d by the way in the crowd ...
...pose it will be necessary for ...
...) Remember the Ladies ...
...ble to them than your ...
...power into the hands of ...
...would be tyrants if the ...
...attention is not paid to ...

*"... and by the way in the new Code of Laws
which I suppose it will be necessary for you to
make I desire you would Remember the Ladies,
and be more generous and favourable to them
than your ancestors. Do not put such unlimited
power into the hands of the Husbands.
Remember all Men would be tyrants if they
could. If perticuliar care and attention is not
paid to the Laidies, we are determined to
foment a Rebelion, and will not hold ourselves
bound by any Laws in which we have no voice,
or Representation.*

*"That your Sex are Naturally Tyrannical is a
Truth so thoroughly established as to admit of
no dispute, but such of you as wish to be happy
willingly give up the harsh title of Master for
the more tender and endearing one of Friend.
Why then, not put it out of the power of the
vicious and the Lawless to use us with cruelty
and indignity with impunity. Men of Sense in
all Ages abhor those customs which treat us
only as the vassals of your Sex. Regard us then
as Beings placed by providence under your
protection and in immitation of the Supreem
Being make use of that power only for our
happiness."*

Remember the Ladies

1750 WOMEN IN AMERICA 1815

LINDA GRANT DE PAUW
CONOVER HUNT

with the assistance of
MIRIAM SCHNEIR

A STUDIO BOOK
THE VIKING PRESS/NEW YORK

Published in association with
The Pilgrim Society

NATIONAL CORPORATE SPONSORS
CLAIROL   PHILIP MORRIS INCORPORATED

NATIONAL BENEFACTORS:
Norton Simon Inc.; Mobil Oil Corporation; National Endowment for the Arts; American Revolution Bicentennial Administration; M. L. Annenberg Foundation; Banks of Plymouth, Massachusetts: Mayflower Cooperative Bank, Plymouth Federal Savings and Loan Association, Plymouth Five Cent Savings Bank, Plymouth-Home National Bank, Plymouth Savings Bank, Rockland Trust Company; Godfrey L. Cabot Trust; Dorothy Jordan Chadwick Fund; Mr. and Mrs. Randolph Kidder; William Randolph Hearst Foundation; Massachusetts Bicentennial Commission; Richard King Mellon Foundation; Plymouth County Development Council, Inc.; Town of Plymouth, Massachusetts.

NATIONAL CORPORATE PATRONS:
Alcoa Foundation; American Express Foundation; American Telephone & Telegraph Company; Barbara Cox Anthony; Elizabeth Arden Inc.; Atlantic Richfield; Borden Inc.; Samuel Bronfman Foundation; Capital Cities Communications, Inc.; CBS Inc.; Anne Cox Chambers; Continental Oil Company; Delta Airlines; Ebony magazine; Exxon Corporation; Famolare, Inc.; Federated Department Stores, Inc.; First National Stores Inc.; Ford Motor Company Fund; Gulf Oil Foundation; Mr. and Mrs. Henry J. Heinz II; IBM Corporation; ITT Corporation; Hecht and Company; The Howard Johnson Foundation; Johnson & Johnson; Warner-Lambert Company; The Lauder Foundation; 3M Company; National Broadcasting Company; Ocean Spray Cranberries, Inc.; Reed & Barton Company; Helena Rubinstein Foundation, Inc.; Saks Fifth Avenue; G. D. Searle & Co.; Sears, Roebuck and Co.; Merrill Lynch, Pierce, Fenner & Smith Inc.; Swift & Company; Union Carbide Corporation; U.S. Steel Corporation; West-Point Pepperell, Inc. (Martex, Lady Pepperell); F. W. Woolworth Company; Radio Station WPLM.

EXHIBITION STAFF:
Mabel H. Brandon,
  National Director
Linda Grant De Pauw, Historian
Conover Hunt, Curator
Miriam Schneir,
  Research Historian
Phyllis Wise, Researcher
Melanie Roher, Design Director
Helen Sokolov, Joan Friedman
  (Educational Exhibitors),
  Design Coordinators
Jules Fisher & Paul Marantz, Inc.,
  Lighting Design
Anita Franks, Executive Secretary
Alison MacTavish, Registrar
Kym Rice, Special Assistant
Mary Lee Berger-Hughes,
  Special Assistant
Stevie Gillespie, Clerical Assistant
Cynthia Krusell, Research Assistant

PARTICIPATING MUSEUMS:
The Pilgrim Hall and The Plymouth
  Antiquarian Society, Plymouth
The High Museum of Art, Atlanta
The Corcoran Gallery of Art,
  Washington, D.C.
The Chicago Historical Society,
  Chicago
The Lyndon Baines Johnson
  Memorial Library, Austin
The New-York Historical Society,
  New York

First published in 1976 by The Viking Press
625 Madison Avenue, New York, N.Y. 10022
Published simultaneously in Canada by
The Macmillan Company of Canada Limited
Printed in the United States of America
Book design by Melanie Roher

Library of Congress Cataloging in Publication Data
De Pauw, Linda Grant.
  "Remember the ladies."
  Bibliography: p.
  1. Women—United States—Social
conditions. 2. United States—History—
1750-1815 3. Women—United States—
History. I. Hunt, Conover, joint author.
II. Schneir, Miriam, joint author. III. Title.
HQ1418.D46   301.41′2′0973   76-14477
ISBN 0-670-59362-1

Contents

Acknowledgments

6

This book and the exhibit on which it is based are an outgrowth of a local project in Plymouth, Massachusetts, to save the home of Mercy Otis Warren from destruction. In less than a year, this initial effort developed into a far more ambitious enterprise, largely through the support of a great many people across the nation—so many, in fact, that we have had to omit scores of names that deserve individual acknowledgment here.

The entire undertaking would have been impossible without the inspiration, leadership, and drive of Muffie Brandon. We are deeply grateful to our lenders and to the staffs of more than a hundred public institutions for their assistance. Despite the pressing demands of their own work in this extraordinary year, they have made it possible for us to assemble—in only four months—the artifacts and documents needed to illuminate the lives and ideas of our Revolutionary forebears. In particular, we would like to acknowledge the assistance of: Mary Black, Curator, The New-York Historical Society, New York; Stella Blum, Curator, The Costume Institute, The Metropolitan Museum of Art, New York; Mary E. Brown, Head of Reader Services, American Antiquarian Society, Worcester, Massachusetts; Georgia B. Bumgardner, Curator of Graphics, American Antiquarian Society, Worcester, Massachusetts; Maud Cole, Keeper of Rare Books, New York Public Library; Julia Finette Davis, Assistant to the Director, Department of Research, Colonial Williamsburg Foundation, Williamsburg, Virginia; David A. Hanks, Curator of American Decorative Arts, Philadelphia Museum of Art; Donald Herold, Director, The Charleston Museum, South Carolina; Gordon Marshall, Assistant Librarian, The Library Company of Philadelphia; Christine Meadows, Curator, Mount Vernon Ladies' Association of the Union, Mount Vernon, Virginia; Peter J. Parker, Curator of Manuscripts, The Historical Society of Pennsylvania, Philadelphia; Charlotte Price, Chief Librarian, Pilgrim Hall, Plymouth, Massachusetts; Fran Silverman, Registrar, Peabody Museum of Archaeology and Ethnology, Harvard University, Cambridge, Massachusetts; Jack C. Spinx, Chief of Exhibitions and Loans, National Gallery of Art, Washington, D.C.; Lillian Tonkin, Reference Librarian, The Library Company of Philadelphia; Caroline J. Weekley, Curator, The Museum of Early Southern Decorative Arts, Winston-Salem, North Carolina; Conrad Wilson, Director, The Chester County Historical Society, West Chester, Pennsylvania.

Among the many private collectors and scholars who helped with the exhibit and the book, special thanks are owed to: Lu Bartlett, Menden Hall, Pennsylvania; Lita Solis-Cohen, Philadelphia; Claire Conway, Librarian, Schwenkfelder Museum, Pennsburg, Pennsylvania; John Demer, Curator, Renfrew Museum, Waynesboro, Pennsylvania; Davida Deutsch, New York; Sandra Downie, Field Curator, Pennsylvania Historical and Museum Commission, Harrisburg, Pennsylvania (for information on Ann Marsh); Wilson H. Fande, Farmington, Connecticut; Cora Ginsburg, Tarrytown, New York; Roy E. Graham, Williamsburg, Virginia; Thomas and Ann Gray, Winston-Salem, North Carolina; Constance Greiff, Heritage Studies, Princeton, New Jersey; Eleanor and Walter Hughes, Boston, Massachusetts; Alvin Josephy, Jr., Editor, American Heritage Magazine, New York; N. F. Karlins, New York (for sharing research on Mary Ann Willson); Kate and Joel Kopp, America Hurrah Antiques, New York; Calder C. Loth, Richmond, Virginia; Florence Montgomery, New Haven, Connecticut; David Pettigrew, George E. Schoelkopf Gallery, New York; Betty Ring, Houston, Texas; Charles Coleman Sellers, Carlisle, Pennsylvania (for information on Patience Lovell Wright); Susan Swan, Assistant Registrar, Winterthur Museum, Winterthur, Delaware; Peter H. Tillou, Litchfield, Connecticut; Charles Van Ravenswaay, Director, Winterthur Museum, Winterthur, Delaware; Jacqui and Julius Sadler, Litchfield, Connecticut; Barbara and William E. Wiltshire III, Richmond, Virginia.

Women's history is a fledgling area of scholarship that has undergone amazing growth within the last decade. We hope that this general survey of women's life and work in the Revolutionary era will stimulate further research into that rich and promising field.

Preface

8

Merely the faintest echo remains in our history books of the extraordinary achievements of women in America in the period 1750-1815. This book, and the exhibition on which much of the material is based, is an attempt to re-examine the historical record. We hope, in so doing, to render credit long overdue to these remarkable women and to enable their history to become an audible theme that will not be lost in generations to follow.

Unfortunately, space does not permit us to mention the many, many kind friends who have helped to make this book and the exhibition a reality. We could not, however, have accomplished this task in such a brief time without the vital assistance of Marjorie Anderson, Ambassador Anne Armstrong, Henry Atkins, Gray Boone, Lucille and William Brewster, J. Carter Brown, Anne Cox Chambers, Joan Gardner, Barbara Gregory, Sir Dennis Hamilton, La Donna Harris, Margaret Heckler, Teresa Heinz, Sherrye Henry, Joan Kennedy, Mrs. Randolph Kidder, Nancy Kissinger, Ann Landers, David Mahoney, Kay Meehan, Constance Mellon, George Olsson, Peter Peterson, James Robinson, Jean Sisco, Carl Stover, Ruth Wakefield, Barbara Walters, Sheila Weidenfeld, Nina Wright, Phyllis Wyeth, and the Women of the Ninety-fourth Congress, as well as our generous sponsors, benefactors, and patrons.

Our thanks is also extended to those remarkable women of the twentieth century who day by day persevered and worked tirelessly against the clock on the exhibition and the book: Peggy Barnett, Mary Lee Berger-Hughes, Joan Friedman, Anita Franks, Stevie Gillespie, Alison MacTavish, Kym Rice, Pam Ridder, Melanie Roher, Sandra Ruch, Miriam Schneir, Helen Sokolov, Carol Sorell, Phyllis Wise, and our patient editors Barbara Burn, Peter Grant, Lewis P. Lewis, Martina D'Alton, and Jacqueline Onassis.

It is our hope that those we could not mention by name will be proud of the results of our combined labors and that our readers will view the women of America of the eighteenth and early nineteenth centuries with new understanding, respect, and justifiable pride.

Mabel H. Brandon
National Director

Introduction

Remember the Ladies...

"Remember the Ladies...," wrote Abigail Adams in 1776. But Americans quickly forgot. In 1840 Charles Francis Adams, the grandson of Abigail, wrote: "The heroism of the females of the Revolution has gone from memory with the generation that witnessed it, and nothing, absolutely nothing remains upon the ear of the young of the present day."

The years between 1750 and 1815 witnessed the passing of a remarkable generation of women who were strong, self-reliant, employed in all occupations entered by men, although not in equal numbers, and active in political and military affairs. Ironically, the conditions that enabled the United States to establish itself as an independent nation and permitted middle-class white men to achieve greater wealth and political power forced women into a more restricted role.

Women were not the only group to experience a regression in status after the Revolution. The American Indians, who were still an important military and political force in the British colonies on the eve of the Revolution, had almost all been forced to leave their homes in the eastern United States within a few decades after Independence. The black population, which made up twenty per cent of those living in the colonies at the time of the Revolution, was forced into a slave system even more repressive than it had been earlier once the invention of the cotton gin in 1793 gave slavery a new economic foundation. America was never a completely egalitarian society, but the gap between the privileged and the unprivileged widened rapidly at the end of the eighteenth century. The tiny proportion of the population—little more than two per cent—that was composed of wealthy ladies and gentlemen of the sort that imported European fashions and ate delicacies such as those served today in "colonial-style" restaurants, grew richer after the war. And the very poor grew poorer.

These developments do not prove that the men and women of our Revolutionary generation were either hypocrites or dupes. Rather they demonstrate that the ideals of the Revolution could not be achieved at a time when industrialization was causing far-reaching changes in the world that no one fully understood or could hope to control. Although the Founding Fathers never intended that slaves, servants, Indians—or women—would share in the freedoms they demanded for themselves, the libertarian ideals they conceived remain a vital legacy. Virtually every American reform movement in the past two hundred years has gone to the Declaration of Independence for its principles.

Life in the early United States was difficult, by our standards, even for the very rich. For women, the ordinary difficulties were compounded by dangerous childbirths, frequent deaths of infants and children, and the ceaseless demands of essential domestic tasks. That so many of them not only coped with these problems but also managed to bring the beauty of needle arts, literature, and painting into their world is a source of pride and inspiration. Their courage and resourcefulness, their contributions to all aspects of the society of their time challenge us to a larger vision of the potential of American women today.

Love and Marriage

There were enormous obstacles to the achievement of love and happiness in eighteenth-century marriages. Marriage was a religious and legal institution, not merely a personal contract. Parents, the church congregation, and, in the case of servants and slaves, owners, regularly broke up potential love matches that they regarded as unsuitable. Some strong-minded individuals, such as John and Abigail Adams, managed to resist the disapproval of others and marry as their hearts dictated. Most, however, such as John and Abigail's children Nabby and John Quincy, bowed to the will of their superiors, put love out of their hearts, and made suitable, passionless marriages, which were often extremely unhappy.

Even for those fortunate enough to be joined to mates they loved, the law and the dictates of moralists concerning the proper behavior of wives operated to prevent the development of a relationship in which husbands and wives could also be friends. Under the English common law, marriage made one person of two, and that person was the husband. Sir William Blackstone, author of *Commentaries on the Law of England* (1765–69), long used as an authority by English and American lawyers, wrote: "By marriage, the husband and wife are one person in law: that is, the very being or legal existence of the woman is suspended during the marriage." The wife lost virtually all rights. She could not legally own any property—not even her own clothing. As Blackstone explained, "A man cannot grant any thing to his wife, or enter into covenant with her: for the grant would be to suppose her separate existence; and to covenant with her, would be only to covenant with himself; and therefore it is also generally true, that all compacts made between husband and wife, when single, are voided by the intermarriage." A wife had no legal rights over her children. She could not sue in court or be sued, and consequently she had difficulty taking legal action against her husband no matter how badly he treated her. In theory, the law gave husbands absolute power over their wives, power even more absolute than the power they had over their servants.

It was this absolute power of husbands that Abigail Adams protested in her famous "Remember the Ladies" letter. She wrote it to her husband to suggest that independence from Great Britain could be made the occasion to put some restrictions on the rights of husbands over their wives. In her letter she pointed out what was certainly true in her husband's case—that men who wished to be happy willingly gave up the rights the laws bestowed upon them and preferred the title "friend" to that of "master." Her lighthearted tone showed that she herself did not fear her husband's theoretical powers. Realizing how little Blackstone had to do with their behavior in their marriage, John Adams, in his reply to his wife's letter, even felt free to tease her a bit about the influence she exerted over him despite her presumably powerless position. He said, "We know better than to repeal our Masculine systems. Altho they are in full Force, you know they are little more than Theory. We dare not exert our Power in its full Latitude. We are obliged to go fair, and softly, and in Practice you know We are the subjects. We have only the Name of Masters, and rather than give up this, which would compleatly subject Us to the Despotism of the Peticoat, I hope General Washington, and all our brave Heroes would fight..." Unfortunately not all husbands loved their wives as passionately or were as consider-

Anonymous, **The Old Maid.** *Engraving, 10-3/16 × 8-3/16 in. London, 1777. Library of Congress, Washington, D.C.*

Colonial society took a dim view of unmarried women, and old maids were thought to be homely, jealous, and foul-tempered. One North Carolina newspaper of 1790 described these hapless spinsters in various terms, calling them "ill-natured, maggotty, peevish, conceited, disagreeable, hypocritical, fretful, noisy, gibing, canting, censorious ... good for nothing creatures." That early marriages were common is evidenced by the powerful William Byrd II of Virginia, who described his beautiful daughter Evelyn as an "antique virgin" when the girl was only twenty.

ate of their wives' opinions and wishes as John Adams. The male domestic tyrants of the eighteenth century could not even conceive of the kind of marital happiness that was possible when a man treated his wife as an equal.

The secret of marital happiness, according to the common knowledge of the eighteenth century, was for the wife to be absolutely obedient to her husband. The advice of Dr. Benjamin Rush to a young woman about to be married was typical. "...from the day you marry you must have no will of your own," he wrote. "The subordination of your sex to ours is enforced by nature, by reason, and by revelation. Of course it must produce the most happiness to both parties. Mr. B. [the intended husband], if he is like others of his sex, will often require unreasonable sacrifices of your will to his. If this should be the case, still honor and obey him.... The happiest marriages I have known have been those when the subordination I have recommended has been most complete."

That such marriages were more likely to bring happiness to husbands than to wives was so obvious that one wonders why women were so anxious to enter into them. Rare indeed was the girl who voluntarily chose to remain single. The views expressed by the schoolgirl Eliza Southgate were hardly typical: "I do esteem marriage absolutely essential to happiness, and that it does not always bring happiness we must every day witness in our acquaintance. A single life is considered too generally as a reproach; but let me ask you, which is the most despicable—she who marries a man she scarcely thinks *well* of—to avoid the reputation of an old maid—or she, who with more delicacy, than marry one she could not highly esteem, preferred to live single all her life.... I congratulate myself that I am at liberty to refuse those I don't like, and that I have firmness enough to brave the sneers of the world and live an old maid, if I never find one I can love." It was generally assumed that any single woman over twenty-five was single because she was so ugly and had such a nasty disposition that no man would have her. A broadside entitled "Old Maid's Last Prayer" reflected the common view:

Come gentle, come simple, come foolish, come witty—
Come don't let me die a maid, take me out of pitty.
I have a sister Sally, she's younger than I am—
She has so many sweethearts she's oblig'd to deny them.
I never was guilty of denying any;
You all know my heart, I'd be thankful for any.

Of course it was not merely fear of ridicule that persuaded young women to marry. The economic system of colonial America was based on households, and individuals who did not marry would generally have to live out their lives as subordinates in someone else's home. Subordination to a husband was preferable to subordination to a father or brother-in-law. And, certainly, like all human beings in all ages, eighteenth-century people longed for the physical and psychological comforts of a home and family.

Henry Drinker, **Valentine.** *Pen and ink, watercolor on cut paper mounted on velvet, 13 in. in diam. Pennsylvania, 1753. Abby Aldrich Rockefeller Folk Art Collection, Williamsburg, Va.*

The ancient custom of sending Valentine greetings was not practiced widely in America until the middle of the 18th century, and then most frequently in Pennsylvania. Henry Drinker, a young Quaker from that colony, sent this greeting to Elizabeth Sandwith nearly eight years before he finally married her in Philadelphia in 1761 after having been married and widowed in the meantime.

Anonymous, **Courtship Fraktur.** *Watercolor and pen on paper, 11-7/8 × 15-1/8 in. framed. Pennsylvania (?), 1800–25. A North Carolina collection. (Photo: Bradford Rauschenberg)*

During the 18th century young couples expressed their sexual attraction with far more freedom than would their later Victorian counterparts. Although the exact symbolism of this courtship drawing eludes modern analysis, the young lady for whom it was intended could hardly have escaped the sexual connotations of the accompanying verse.

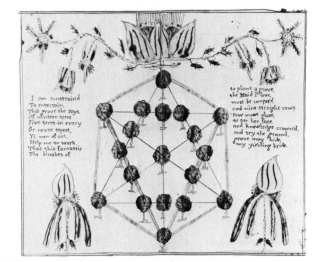

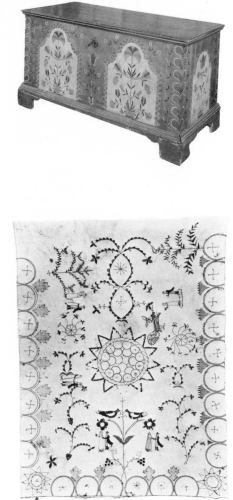

Americans of the mid-eighteenth century frankly recognized the attraction between the sexes. "Dear Madam," John Adams wrote to Abigail while he was courting her, "every experimental Phylosopher knows, that the steel and the magnet or the Glass and feather will not fly together with more Celerity, than somebody And somebody, when brought within the striking Distance." European visitors were astonished by the freedom with which American young people "sparked." The Marquis de Chastellux, observing a courting couple holding hands in public, remarked on "the extreme liberty that prevails in this country between the two sexes, as long as they are not married. It is no crime for a girl to kiss a young man." That they often went a good way beyond kissing is evident from the large number of first babies born seven months or less after a couple's wedding day.

Toward the end of the eighteenth century the sexual attitudes of upperclass and "respectable" middle-class people became much more inhibited, and in the nineteenth century sexual prudishness increased among the lower class and slave population as well. An illustration of the changing attitudes is the attack on the courting custom known as "bundling." In the early part of the century, for a couple to cuddle together in bed with their clothes on was considered a perfectly proper way for them to get to know each other better, but gradually it became a practice confined to the country folk, and those who indulged in it were described as "guilty."

As attitudes toward sex grew more repressed, the difficulty of achieving happiness in marriage increased still further. Courtship, particularly among the upper classes, developed into a kind of teasing game. Young ladies strove to lead as many young men as possible into declaring their love, while at the same time appearing to give them no encouragement whatever. When a young man proposed marriage, the young woman must pretend to be surprised, embarrassed, a little bit angry, and must always turn him down—at least the first time. How long she dangled him on the hook depended on how well she played the game and how much she enjoyed it. Eventually, of course, she must marry and from then on cease flirtation and be totally obedient and faithful to her husband. Courting practices in which so much dishonesty was involved did not encourage frankness and mutual understanding in marriage.

Houses of prostitution existed in many American cities by the end of the century. When theaters were built a special gallery was reserved for "loose women" and their clients. In both North and South the prostitutes were usually white women. Women who had been "ruined," because of rape during the Revolution or because the young man they expected to marry deserted them, would feel obliged to leave home to save their parents from disgrace. And as job opportunities for women narrowed, prostitution was viewed as an alternative to starvation.

Opposite, above: **Chest.** *Painted pine, 25 × 37-3/4 × 22-1/2 in. Berks County (?), Pennsylvania, c. 1790. Private collection. (Photo: Ron Jennings)*

Pennsylvania Germans carried many Old World customs with them to the New World. In colonial America marriageable daughters were expected to bring dowries to their future husbands, and chests were among the most common articles taken by brides into their first homes.

Opposite, below: **Coverlet.** *Wool crewels on linen, 92 × 71 in., including fringe. Pennsylvania, c. 1810. Kate and Joel Kopp, America Hurrah Antiques, New York.*

The unidentified woman who embroidered this coverlet left a decidedly puzzling needlework record of relationships between the sexes. Within a symbolic framework of flowers, birds, plants, and animals, she placed two figures – a man and a woman – who move around the surface in a counterclockwise journey that ends in old age. The exact symbolism of the groupings remains elusive, a problem compounded by the unexpected presence of a monster yelling, "Boo Hoo," as it is stung by an insect.

Left: Anonymous, Frontispiece engraving from the 13th ed. of Aristotle (pseudonym), **Aristotle's Complete Master-Piece, in three parts, Displaying the Secrets of Nature in the Generation of Man....** *5-1/2 × 3-3/8 in. [Philadelphia, M. Cary], 1796. The Library Company of Philadelphia. (Photo: Joseph Kelley)*

First published in England during the 17th century, this pocket-size sex manual sold widely in numerous editions on both sides of the Atlantic until the second quarter of the 19th century.

*Opposite: Anonymous, **The Old Plantation.** Watercolor on paper, 16 × 20 in. framed. Found in South Carolina, c. 1800. Abby Aldrich Rockefeller Folk Art Collection, Williamsburg, Va.*

Despite Christianizing influences, African slaves retained many of their tribal customs in America. This lively dance, which may record a slave wedding, shows dance steps that reflect African influence. Tribal dances often incorporated the use of canes and scarves; bandanas, called "head ties," were tied and colored in ways that indicated status. The blue-and-white head scarves shown here resemble West African Yoruba cloth. One musician plays an African molo, a precursor of the banjo, while another taps a percussion instrument identified as a gudu-gudu drum.

The African attitudes toward sex and marriage differed from those of the white Americans. But since the Africans came to America as slaves, their masters' views forced them to change or at least modify their own. In the early years of slavery, men so greatly outnumbered women that family relationships were virtually impossible. By the middle of the eighteenth century, however, the sexes were nearly balanced, and the masters encouraged monogamous marriages by their slaves. Masters believed, with some cause, that married slaves would make less trouble, would work harder, and were less likely to run away. They were also glad to see slave children born to add to their property. In early America slaves, like their white owners, could court quite freely, and unlike white girls, black girls were almost always allowed to marry for love. Slave parents did not have the authority to forbid a child's marriage, and the master was usually content to have his slaves choose their own partners. If slaves did not find partners soon enough to suit the master or if they chose someone from another plantation, which the master feared would encourage them to run away, the master might arrange a marriage. Such arrangements might be particularly unhappy because of the contrast with the usual love matches. Slave marriage ceremonies were performed by the master, by a white minister, or by a black preacher. Since slave marriages could always be dissolved by the sale of one of the parties, the words spoken never included the phrase "till death us do part," nor was any reference made to the inappropriate command that no man should put asunder whom God had joined together. On some plantations owners felt so uncomfortable about having their slaves married in a ceremony closely approximating the white ritual that they performed "broomstick marriages," in which the couple was made to jump a broomstick to complete the formalities. But other owners enjoyed slave weddings as a chance for a party, and field slaves as well as house slaves might be given elaborate weddings complete with a cake and a white veil for the bride. Such white-style weddings, however, only gradually replaced ceremonies and celebrations in which slaves employed dances and traditions remembered from their African heritage.

White upper-class people found it extremely difficult to end a marriage except by death. Petitions to colonial legislatures by either spouse might result in dissolution of the marriage. When two people who disliked each other were unable to divorce, dislike could grow to murderous hatred, and tales of inhuman cruelty of wives toward husbands as well as of husbands toward wives abound. Bathsheba Spooner, daughter of a prominent Massachusetts family, was convicted of murdering her husband in 1778. Before her execution she explained "that her match with her husband was not agreeable to her. Domestic dissentions soon took place, and went on from step to step, till she conceived an utter aversion to him; at length she meditated his destruction; laid several plans, and never gave over till the fatal act was committed."

COURTSHIP AND MARRIAGE.

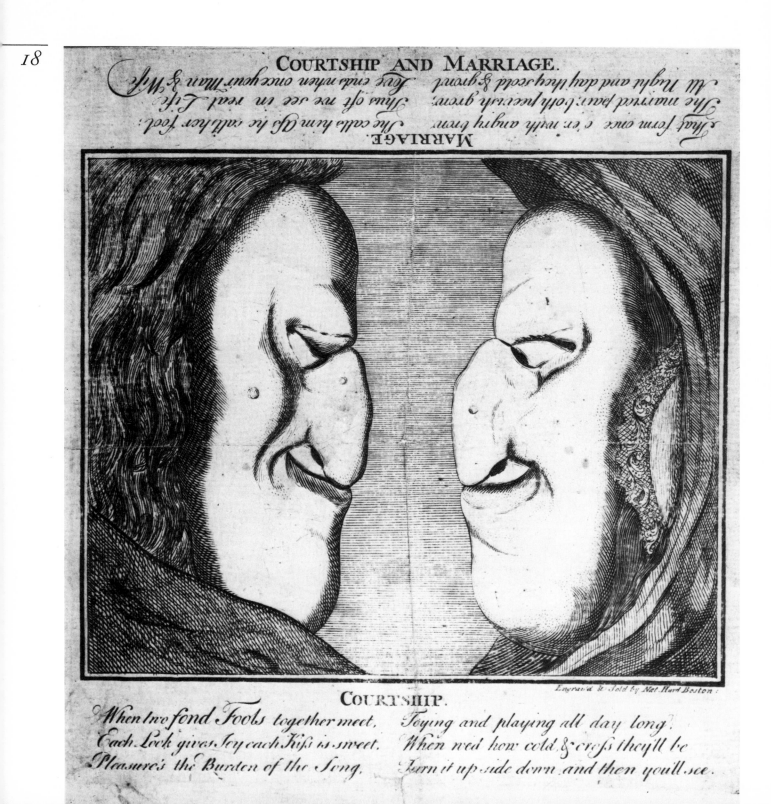

MARRIAGE.

That form once e'er with angry brow, *The married pair both leerish grow,*
She calls him Ass he calls her fool; *All Night and day they scold & growl,*
Thus oft we see in real Life, *Love ends when once your Man & Wife.*

Engrav'd & Sold by Nat. Hurd Boston.

COURTSHIP.

When two fond Fools together meet,   *Toying and playing all day long.*
Each Look gives Joy each Kiss is sweet.   *When wed how cold & cross they'll be*
Pleasure's the Burden of the Song.   *Turn it up side down and then you'll see.*

The attitudes of the east coast Indians toward sex and marriage were in general simpler than those of the European colonists. So long as two young people were attracted to each other and were not members of the same family group, there would be no obstacle to their marriage. Sometimes, of course, one young person would love another who did not reciprocate. If wooing, love songs, and love charms did not work, those disappointed in love would occasionally kill themselves. But usually an Indian courtship had a happy ending. Marriage among most of the eastern American tribes had neither religious nor legal significance. It often involved nothing more than the couple beginning to sleep together. Some tribes even permitted trial marriages. Chastity was not required before marriage, but adultery was a serious crime. Indian divorces were easily arranged but rare, especially if there were children. Rape was virtually unknown, and prostitution developed only after the Indians discovered that white men would pay to sleep with a woman. Indian marriages seem generally to have been happy. It is significant that white women, raised in an alien culture, often preferred life with the Indians when they were captured and adopted into a tribe. They were encouraged but not forced to marry, and they often came to love their Indian husbands and families more than those they had left behind. Mary Jemison, who was captured by the Shawnee Indians in 1755 and married a Delaware when she was seventeen, told the white colonists that her husband was "good, tender, generous," and that "strange as it may seem, I loved him."

Nevertheless, despite all the obstacles, there were some outstandingly happy and successful marriages in eighteenth-century America, marriages in which the wife as well as the husband felt loved and cherished. And although most marriages were cut short by the premature death of one partner, some endured for fifty years or more. Such a marriage was that of John and Abigail Adams. After many years as a wife, Abigail Adams could write to her husband, "the age of romance has long ago past, but the affection of almost Infant years has matured and strengthend untill it has become a vital principle."

*Opposite: Nathaniel Hurd, **Courtship and Marriage**. Engraving, 9 × 8 in. Boston, 1760–75. American Antiquarian Society, Worcester, Mass.*

This amusing trompe-l'oeil print offers a view of marriage shared by countless 18th-century Americans, who felt that wedlock meant the end of a beautiful relationship between the sexes. Beneath the faces representing Courtship, Hurd applauds the naive happiness of the chase: "when two fond Fools together meet./Each Look gives Joy each Kiss is sweet." However, the companion view of Marriage strikes a more dour tone: "All night and day they scold & growl/ She calls him Ass he calls her fool./Thus oft we see in Real Life/Love ends when once your Man & Wife."

Motherhood

For women in pre-Revolutionary America, marriage was generally followed by an uninterrupted series of pregnancies throughout the childbearing years. The birth rate in the white population in the mid-eighteenth century was as high as it is today anywhere in the world. Before the Revolution the population doubled every generation. The practice of marrying young and bearing as many children as possible was a deviation from European patterns. In Europe at that time about one-fifth of the population never married at all, and those who did often delayed marriage until their late twenties. A combination of malnutrition and prolonged nursing acted as natural contraceptives, so that women bore children at intervals of twenty-five to thirty months and rarely had more than four or five. In America, however, almost everyone married, and the shortage of women resulted in marriage at an early age. Large families were considered an advantage and were far more common than small ones.

After the middle of the eighteenth century the great imbalance between men and women in the population gradually lessened. As the ratio approached a normal level, the statistics on males in marriage remained the same, but the women apparently began to marry later, widows remarried less frequently, the number of spinsters increased, and the birth rate began to decline. At the same time, for reasons that are not clear, there were perceptible changes in attitudes toward child-rearing, with a far greater emphasis on a child's need for love and nurture by its mother.

The declining birth rate among white Americans was partly the result of the reduction of the number of women who were wives. But colonial Americans also learned to practice birth control; the usual method was withdrawal, and they also knew ways of producing abortions. This lore was generally conveyed orally and rarely committed to writing. Much was probably learned from the native American women. The east coast Indians customarily had families limited to two children and looked to the adoption of captives taken in war rather than to natural increase to maintain the numbers of the tribe when population declined because of war or disease. In order to assure a good supply of milk for each child American tribes believed it necessary to abstain from intercourse for a period after childbirth. This period ranged from a few months to as long as three or four years, which was the practice among the Sioux. Early observers declared that Indian women had medicines that produced temporary sterility and others that caused abortion. Most likely it was the Indians who discovered that the root of Black Cohosh *(Cimicifuga)*, an indigenous plant, would cause pregnant women to abort. Ergot, a fungus that grows on rye and that was used by midwives to hasten a slow labor, was another substance that could be used to cause abortion. By the turn of the nineteenth century abortion had become so common among American women that at least one doctor felt it necessary to warn them against the practice. Writing in 1804, Dr. William Buchan stated: "I am sorry to think that any awful warning should be necessary to check the commission of so wicked an outrage upon nature, as an attempt to procure abortion. This can never be effected without either the probable death of the mother, or the certain ruin of her constitution; the stimulants which are used to force the womb prematurely to discharge its sacred deposit, must inflame the parts so as to cause a mortification."

Opposite, above:
Obstetric Case with Tools. *Leather, brass, wood, steel, 2-1/2 × 18-1/4 × 19-1/2 in. (open). Europe, c. 1780. Smithsonian Institution, Washington, D.C. (Photo: Ray Schwartz)*

Opposite, below:
Easy chair ... useful for lying-in women and sick persons. *Engraved illustration (Plate I) from Charles White,* **A Treatise on the Management of Pregnant and Lying in Women and the Means of Curing, but more especially of Preventing the principal Disorders to which they are liable.** *8-1/2 × 5-1/4 in. Worcester, Massachusetts, Isaiah Thomas, 1793. The Library Company of Philadelphia. (Photo: Joseph Kelley)*

Below:
Maternity Dress. *Linen. Chester County, Pennsylvania, 1740–90. Philadelphia Museum of Art. (Photo: Will Brown)*

Everyday homespun dresses of the 18th century are rare, and maternity clothes even more so. The unknown woman who made this simple blue-and-white striped dress added an expandable waist and bodice to accommodate her pregnancy; at other times the dress could be drawn in to fit her slender figure.

The medical care of pregnant women, including those suffering from such "female complaints" as an unwanted pregnancy, was almost exclusively in the hands of midwives. Many of these women presided at thousands of births, and some had studied with male physicians at European universities. Male midwives were virtually unknown in America until the last part of the eighteenth century. Women were long preferred because of their greater experience and presumably greater intuitive knowledge of childbirth. An early-eighteenth-century manual for midwives described the ideal midwife thus: "She should be young, and vigorous, learned in her art, able to take all-night vigils, strong of arms and hands for difficult cases of turning and extraction.... She must have slender hands, long fingers, tender feelings, sympathy, be hopeful, and above all, silent." The male author of the manual explained that he had learned a great deal from "old women" and that other men might too, "if they were not too obstinate." The same author denounced the "new and unnatural forceps, and the unseemly haste with which they are often applied."

As the century advanced, midwives were accustomed to use forceps, but only in cases where it appeared that the mother's life might be lost without them. A midwives' manual written by Dr. William Smellie and reprinted in Boston in 1786, *An Abridgement of the Practice of Midwifery*, contained an illustration of a pair of obstetrical forceps with the following explanation: "The handles and the lowest part of the Blades may as here be covered with any durable Leather, but the Blades ought to be wrapped round with something of a thinner kind, which may be easily renewed when there is the least suspicion of venereal Infection in a former Case; by being thus covered, the Forceps have a better hold, and mark less the Head of the Child. For their easier Introduction, the Blades ought likewise to be greased with Hog's-lard."

In 1765 Dr. William Shippen, Jr., opened a maternity ward and lectured on midwifery in Philadelphia, which led to the founding of the University of Pennsylvania Medical School, the first medical school in America. In his newspaper advertisement for students, he declared that he had felt it his duty to offer the course after "having been lately called to the assistance of a number of women in the country, in difficult labors, most of which was made so by the unskillful old women about them." His course, he said, was prepared "to instruct those women who have virtue enough to own their ignorance and apply for instructions, as well as those young gentlemen now engaged in the study of that useful and necessary branch of surgery, who are taking pains to qualify themselves." Some women did take advantage of Dr. Shippen's instruction. In 1789 Grace Mulligan announced that she would soon begin practice as a midwife in Wilmington, Delaware, after studying with "Dr. Shippen in Philadelphia better than a year." Women midwives vastly outnumbered men until after 1780. Then, as women were excluded from the new medical schools, men soon drove them from the profession, so that eventually women delivered babies only in remote areas or among the poor.

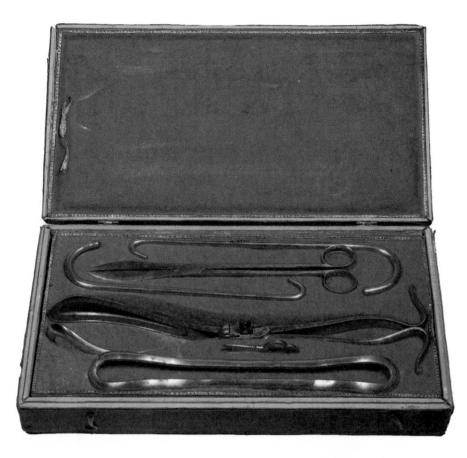

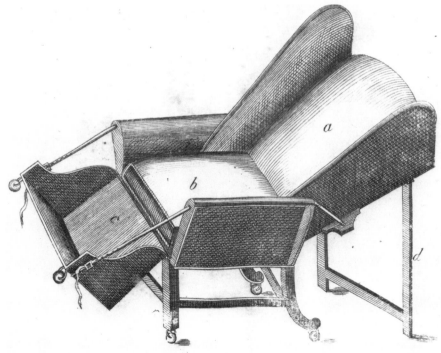

Advertisement for Mary Bass, Midwife, from **The Essex** *(Massachusetts)* **Gazette,** *July 14–21, 1772. New York Public Library.*

Pregnancy and childbirth were replete with dangers for colonial women, and complications could permanently damage a mother's health and frequently caused her death. For unmarried mothers, the hardships were multiplied. Eighteenth-century society was tolerant of brides who were pregnant on their wedding day, but a young woman who became pregnant and then found that her lover refused to marry her faced public disgrace and punishment. If she was willing to identify the father, he would be forced to pay for the maintenance of the child. If she was a servant, her term of service would be increased. The black slave society was more tolerant of unwed mothers. The master generally did not care who had fathered the infants in the slave quarters, and the slaves well understood the pressures that might be brought to bear on a slave girl by overseers and other white men. They would not add to her suffering by ostracizing her or her baby. The native Americans generally lacked the concept of illegitimacy. So long as there was no incest involved, there was no stigma attached to either an unwed mother or her child. Many tribes, including the Mandan and the Arikara, even had a type of religious rite in which women were required to take new partners for a period of time. One of General Braddock's soldiers described such an event while observing the Indians at Fort Cumberland during the French and Indian War: "It is the custom with them, once or twice a year, for the women to dance and all the men to sit by.... Each woman takes out her man that she likes, dances with him, and lies with him for a week, and then [they] return to their former husbands and live as they did before." It was a rule in these rites that no woman could choose her own husband, but it was noted that some women deliberately chose very old men. These practices were not considered adultery.

Left: "Ehre Vater Artist" (attrib.), **Birth and Baptismal Certificate of Sarah Zimmerman** *(born in Friedland, N.C., March 10, 1777). Watercolor and ink on paper, 15-3/8 × 12-3/4 in. North Carolina, 1800–10. Old Salem, Inc., Winston-Salem, N.C. (Photo: Bradford Rauschenberg)*

Germans in America often commissioned illuminated **Taufcheine** *to record the birth and baptismal dates of their children. This lively example bears the hand of more than one artist and must have been made in advance of the commission, for the circular legend at the bottom reads: "It is a commendable thing for a boy to apply his mind to the study of good letters; they will always be useful to him; they will procure him the love and favour of good men, which those that are wise, value more than riches and pleasure."*

Opposite: Joseph Sympson, Jr., after William Hogarth, **A Woman Swearing a Child to a Grave Citizen.** *Etching and engraving, 12 × 14 in. London, 1730–35. Anglo-American Art Museum, Louisiana State University, Baton Rouge.*

During the 18th century illegitimacy was a problem on both sides of the Atlantic. Bastard children placed a burden on local governments unless the financial responsibility could be passed on to the father. The print shown here illustrates the difficulty sometimes encountered in identifying the male parent.

Right: **Child's Moccasins.** *Deerskin embroidered with porcupine quills and tufts of dyed deer hair, 5-1/2 × 3-3/4 in. Iroquois, late 18th century. Peabody Museum of Archaeology and Ethnology, Cambridge, Mass. Gift of the Misses Palfrey. (Photo: Hillel Burger)*

The tree design on the ankle flaps and instep is typical of Iroquois work.

Below: **Child's Dress.** *Wool crewels on linen, 37 in. America, 18th century. Wadsworth Atheneum, Hartford, Conn. Gift of Mrs. Charles B. Salisbury.*

Every Indian baby, no matter who the father was, had a place in its mother's family group. In the white society, however, unwed mothers might be driven to kill the child and perhaps themselves as well. A broadside published in 1771 drew a moral lesson from the experience of a young woman who drowned herself in the Medford River:

> Now unto you I shall relate
> The awful and surprizeing fate
> Of a fair Maid, both Young and Gay:
> Who Liv'd in Malden, as they say....
> Became with child, as I believe,
> By one who did her much Decieve
> For he had promis'd as they said:
> Quickly to marry this Young Maid....
> I pray it may a warning be
> To old and young, to bond and free,
> To see how Sin it blinds our eyes,
> Makes us our Maker to despise....

A Boston newspaper reported on April 17, 1755: "Last Thursday Night a young Woman at Watertown about 20 Years of Age was delivered by her self of a Child which she destroyed by throwing it into a Well, where it was found the next Day, with some Marks of Violence upon it. At present she is kept under a Guard till she can with safety be removed to Gaol."

Infanticide in eighteenth-century America was less prevalent than it was in contemporary England and probably decreased in the last part of the century. Nevertheless, the rate of child mortality was appallingly high in the eighteenth century, and its marked decline in the early nineteenth century suggests that certain features of colonial child-rearing practices indirectly caused many of the deaths. Many things colonial mothers did to their babies presumably for their own good proved fatal. For instance, colonial mothers greatly respected John Locke's *Thoughts on Education,* published in England in 1690. Although it was generally agreed that washing more than hands and face could damage the health of an adult, John Locke recommended icy baths for infants and young children. Josiah Quincy, who was reared in eastern Massachusetts, recalled that in winter as well as summer he would be carried from his warm bed and taken to a cellar kitchen to be dipped three times in a tub of frigid water straight from the well. Also in keeping with Locke's advice, his shoes were made with thin soles so that water could leak in. In his boyhood, he said, he spent most of his time with cold, wet feet. Quincy survived this treatment; many of his generation did not.

HUSH a by Baby
On the Tree Top,
When the Wind blows
The Cradle will rock ;
When the Bough breaks
The Cradle will fall,
Down tumbles Baby,
Cradle and all.

*Woodcut from **Mother Goose's Melody: or Sonnets for the Cradle.** 4 × 2-5/8 in. Massachusetts, Isaiah Thomas, 1794. American Antiquarian Society, Worcester, Mass.*

*Matthew Harris Jouett, **Mrs. Matthew Harris Jouett** [Margaret Henderson Allen] **and George Payne Jouett**. Oil on wood, 26 × 20-1/2 in. Kentucky, 1814. Mrs. James Ross Todd.*

*Opposite: Henry Inman, after Charles Bird King, **Portrait of a** [Chippewa] **Squaw and Child**. Oil on canvas, 38 × 33 in. America, c. 1830–40. Courtesy Peabody Museum of Archaeology and Ethnology, Cambridge, Mass. (Photo: Hillel Burger)*

In the early part of the eighteenth century infants were swaddled in linen bands, which parents thought would keep their naturally bowed legs straight and so help them grow normally. Swaddling bands caused babies to sleep more and prevented them from soiling clothing and beds. Both boys and girls wore skirts as infants, usually of washable linen; slave boys were kept in short shirts without pants into their teens, but white children began to dress as their parents did at the age of six or seven. Wealthy little ladies as young as three were dressed in silk shoes with high heels that must have made toddling quite difficult. Young girls of five wore stays, and even little boys in their frocks and petticoats were braced up with whalebone and buckram. The passage from children's clothing to adult costume was more clear-cut for boys than for girls, since they abandoned dresses for more manly attire, but upper-class adult clothing was uncomfortable for both sexes. Happily, less than three per cent of the population was of such exalted rank that they had to submit to these European fashions. Lower-class children wore plainer, more comfortable clothing appropriate to their social status.

Indian babies spent their early lives in cradleboards. The Iroquois, Algonquian and other eastern tribes made these of thin rectangular boards brightly painted. Some had footrests. Soft shredded bark or similar material was placed between the baby's legs as a diaper and a fawn skin wrapped over that. Various objects might be suspended from cradleboards, such as squirrel tails, turkey feathers, or shells. Some of these were protective charms while others served simply to amuse the baby. A cradleboard could be hung from a pole to keep an infant out of danger and was easily transported. Indian babies were permanently confined in cradleboards only when they were very small; as soon as they could crawl or toddle they were encouraged to romp about, usually in a minimum of clothing.

The colonial baby's first food was its mother's milk. But if, as all too often happened, the mother had died in childbirth or was too ill to nurse, the child would either be fed by a wet nurse or from a bottle. A variety of substances, including ceramic, silver, and even the dangerous lead-based pewter, was used for nursing bottles and nipples. These were cold, hard substances that made a poor substitute for a mother's breast. After the child was weaned, parents who followed John Locke's advice would not feed it meat until it was several years old. Instead children might have brown bread, corn puddings, baked beans, and perhaps milk and cheese. The beverage Locke recommended for little children was warm beer, since it was considered unhealthy to drink water. He disapproved of most fruit, and mothers were cautioned not to feed youngsters melons, peaches, plums, or grapes, although berries, ripe pears, and apples were acceptable.

Middle-class children ate their food from wooden or pewter bowls, often with their fingers, while wealthy tots might have silver bowls, cups, and spoons.

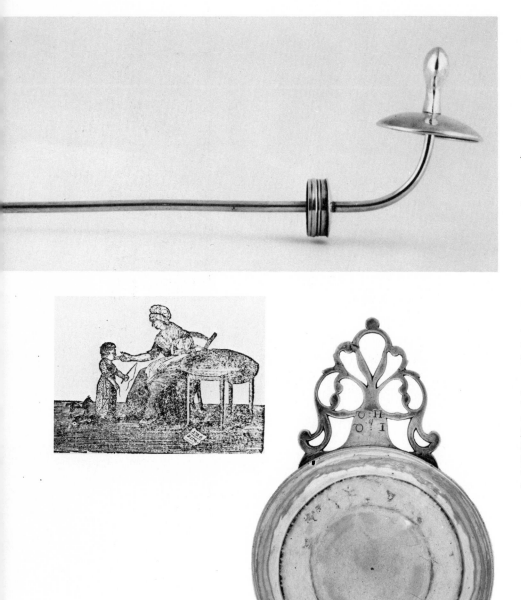

Left: John McMullin, **Nipple and Tube** (for insertion in a glass nursing bottle). Silver, 7-7/16 in. Philadelphia, Pennsylvania, 1795–1800. Museum of Fine Arts, Boston, Spaulding Collection.

Many early nursing bottles had metal nipples and tubes that must have irritated babies' mouths and were also extremely difficult to clean. The use of poisonous lead-based pewter for some nursing bottles did little to reduce the incidence of infant mortality and sickness.

Below, left:
Mother Nursing. Woodcut from William Darton, **A Present for a Little Girl.** Baltimore, Warner and Hanna, 1806. American Antiquarian Society, Worcester, Mass.

Below:
William Homes, **Child's Porringer.** Silver, 1-3/4 × 6-1/8 in. Boston, Massachusetts, 1740–70. Museum of Fine Arts, Boston. Bequest of Miss Grace W. Treadwell.

Most American children ate from simple wooden bowls; however, the youthful gentry sometimes enjoyed their gruel in silver porringers. This example was presented as a gift from Josiah Quincy of Massachusetts to either his daughter-in-law, Hannah (wife of Samuel Quincy), or his granddaughter, Hannah Quincy, born in 1763.

Opposite:
Paper Doll, from **The History of Little Fanny, Exemplified in a Series of Figures.** 4-1/2 × 3-5/8 in. Boston, J. Belcher, 1812. American Antiquarian Society, Worcester, Mass.

This moralistic children's tale illustrated with cutouts describes the woes of a willful girl who disobeys her mother and suffers the consequences.

Both Indians and Africans believed in prolonged nursing, sometimes until a child was three or four. As in many other areas, the slaves were prevented from putting their beliefs into practice by owners who thought their ways were better. The American Indians, however, raised their children differently from Europeans. An early observer said of the Texas Indians, "Those people love their offspring the most of any in the world, and treat them with the greatest mildness." This description might have been applied to all American tribes. Indians never beat their children; indeed even mild physical punishment was virtually unknown. Loud scoldings were almost as rare. The Indians depended on persuasion and good examples to develop the traits of character they considered desirable, and by all accounts these methods were quite effective.

In the first part of the eighteenth century colonial parents were often indifferent to their children until they reached the age of reason. A poem printed in England in 1775 rebuked parents who still:

>Rank their children, in their earliest years,
>Among their cats and dogs, their bulls and bears;
>Mere animals whose gambols now and then
>May raise a laugh, and turn the rising spleen
>Ere reason dawn'd, or Cunning Learnt disguise.

Perhaps when so many children died as infants it would have been intolerable for parents to become warmly attached to their offspring until they were old enough to have a reasonable chance of survival. In the second half of the century, parents began to pay more attention to their children, which in some families meant an emphasis on discipline and breaking the child's will. One parent who practiced such child-rearing methods proudly wrote, "My children from the youngest to the eldest loves me and fears me as sinners dread death. My look is law." But as the century wore on, American parents began to cultivate the love of their children through gentleness and affection, and both men and women spoke of the joys of raising a family.

Parents did not abandon the rod when their attitudes toward their children softened, but they tried to make the education of their children a less unpleasant experience. The early education of the young was largely in the hands of mothers. They were taught some useful work such as spinning or knitting, while still toddlers. Mothers were expected to give their children moral instruction and, if possible, to teach them to read their Bible. Some mothers also taught their offspring to write with ink and quill pens, and a well-educated woman might even begin a child's education in Greek and Latin at home.

Mothers who did not have much time to spare for their children's education might send them to local schools, where they learned the basic skills of sewing and reading from a woman who made teaching her business. The first reading lesson often came from a hornbook, which displayed an alphabet and the Lord's Prayer printed on a board protected from little fingers by transparent horn. Early primers, such as *The New-England Primer,* came next and contained reading exercises on moral themes and a catechism, so that children could learn their

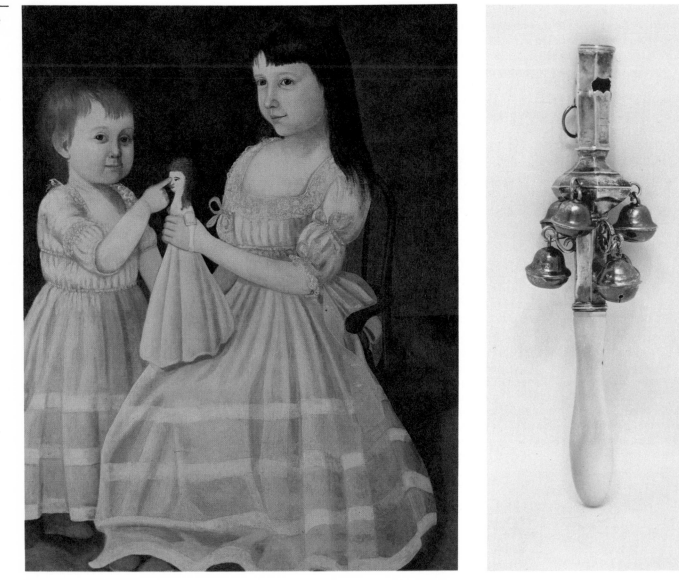

letters as they received religious training. Early primers dwelt heavily on the subject of death in a way that modern child-rearing experts might find unwholesome. "Now I lay me down to sleep," read the colonial children in *The New-England Primer*, "I pray the Lord my soul to keep. If I should die before I wake, I pray the Lord my soul to take." Not until after the Revolution did books for children lose this grim tone and begin to present lessons in a form designed to please and amuse the child.

Toys were an expensive luxury, whether purchased or made by hand at home. Colonial children were encouraged to work hard and were discouraged from wasting their time in play, but every little girl probably had some sort of doll, even if it was simply an old corncob or stick and resembled a baby only in the mind of its little mother. Playing with a doll was approved, for it would help a girl to learn some necessary skills. Wealthy children might have doll furniture and toy coaches as well as expensive imported dolls.

Indian mothers made elaborate dolls for their daughters using such materials as wood, clay, animal skins, and real human hair. The faces would be painted in imitation of the cosmetic style favored by the mother and facial and body tattoos would be copied. The dolls had clothing, jewelry and hair styles to conform to tribal tastes, and they had miniature cradleboards, dishes, and tepees for playing "house." Little girls who were not satisfied with such dolls might dress puppies and put them into cradleboards. Indian fathers made miniature bows and arrows for their sons to play with. Indian children also enjoyed tops, skates made of rib bones, and balls.

White boys had marbles and jackknives, and there were various sorts of rattles for infants, ranging from a dried gourd to an elaborate silver rattle with bells. When children played, however, they were more likely to play games than to play with toys. Large families meant there was always a crowd of children to play such games as tag and "thread the needle," as well as a number of popular singing games, including some, like "London Bridge Is Falling Down," that are still played today. But colonial children also knew games that are no longer played. An early children's book called *The Pretty Little Pocket Book* gives the rules for playing games in rhyme. One of these, called "Pitch and Hussel," is described thus:

> Poise your hand fairly
> Pitch plumb your Slat.
> Then shake for all Heads
> Turn down the Hat.

As child-rearing practices in the last half of the eighteenth century grew milder, the greater attention given to the education and well-being of children made greater demands on the mother, but it also made mothering a far more satisfying experience than it had been in the days before the Revolution.

*Opposite, left: Reuben Moulthrop (attrib.), **Elizabeth and Mary Daggert**. Oil on canvas, 36 × 28-1/2 in. Connecticut, c. 1794. The Connecticut Historical Society, Hartford.*

*Opposite, right: Philip Syng, Jr., **Child's Whistle and Bells.** Silver and mother-of-pearl, 6 in. Philadelphia, Pennsylvania, c. 1750. Museum of Fine Arts, Boston. Bequest of Samuel A. Green.*

At a time when large families and frugal living were the general rule, few Americans could afford to pamper their children with elegant toys and playthings. The luxury of teething on a silver and mother-of-pearl whistle like this one was reserved for infants born into the wealthiest segment of American society.

Sickness and Death

In colonial America, only the exceptional person lived long enough to die of old age. About 1790 Dr. Benjamin Rush, one of the most prominent physicians in the country, compiled some statistics based on his own long experience in Philadelphia that reflect a shocking mortality rate. Of one hundred people born in any given year in Philadelphia, Dr. Rush found at the end of

Years	Remained Alive
6	64
16	46
26	26
36	16
46	10
56	6
66	3
76	1

In addition to complications of pregnancy and accidents—including deaths by violence in war or as punishment for crime—the population of America was exposed to a chamber of horrors of diseases, most of which have become so rare today that even doctors may never see an active case.

For eighteenth-century Americans, the primary threat to health and life was infectious disease. As the human populations of three continents mingled, diseases endemic to Europe, Africa, and America spread, and entirely new diseases developed. Yellow fever and pernicious malaria, for instance, were new to the European colonists, and they had no immunity. Both scarlet fever and diphtheria were in a process of evolution in the eighteenth century; diphtheria had been a mild disease before 1735, when it suddenly assumed a fatal form in an outbreak in Kingston, New Hampshire. Not a single one of the first forty victims recovered. Measles, whooping cough, and dysentery attacked the white, black, and red populations alike, while the blacks seemed particularly susceptible to pulmonary diseases—influenza, tuberculosis, and pleurisy—and the Indians were defenseless against smallpox.

Smallpox was probably the most dreaded disease of the eighteenth century. One of the most highly contagious of all diseases, it spread alarmingly wherever there were large numbers of unvaccinated people. Once it appeared, nearly every exposed person who had not been vaccinated or had not had the disease before was virtually certain to contract it. The mortality rate varied, but in the white population of colonial America one victim in every seven or eight died. Among the blacks, the proportion was slightly lower, since the disease had been endemic in Africa even longer than in Europe, but among the Indians it was much higher. The death rate in eastern tribes was rarely as low as fifty per cent, and some groups were entirely destroyed by the disease. When the disease did not kill, it left its victim covered with deep pitted scars that caused disfiguration for life.

Ironically, the efforts that were made to cure disease may actually have decreased the chances of survival. "More die of the practitioner than of the natural course of the disease," wrote an English physician who had studied conditions in North America. And the more highly educated the doctor, the faster and more painfully was the patient likely to die. In both England and America surgeons were considered craftsmen, not professionals. The men and women who practiced as barbers worked as surgeons as well—setting bones, performing amputations, cutting ulcers and boils, and treating wounds with neither anesthetics nor any interest in cleanliness. Seventy per cent of their compound fracture cases died. University-trained physicians, whose education was wholly theoretical, were rare in America. It has been estimated that of approximately thirty-five hundred men who practiced medicine in America at the time of the Revolution only four hundred had an M.D. degree. Of the much larger number of women who practiced medicine, even a smaller number had had formal training. Those who learned from experience, however, were usually preferred by patients, with good reason.

Whatever a patient's complaint, the aim of the physician was to get out the "vile humours" that were causing illness. These were thought to be harbored in the stomach, the intestines, or the blood, and the treatments were vomiting, purging, and bleeding. The drugs most frequently prescribed were calomel, mercury, opium, ipecac, rattlesnake root, and Jesuit's bark, and all were used in very large, if inexactly measured, quantities. Bleeding, with a blade and bowl or with live leeches, was no doubt often the immediate cause of a patient's death, since it was common to take forty ounces of blood or even more. Some prescriptions called for bleeding a patient of more blood than is now known to exist in the whole body. The notion was that when the hot, fever-producing blood was drained, there would be nothing left for the disease to work on and it would depart. It usually did—along with the patient's life.

These educated doctors and those influenced by them sneered at the remedies of "old women," which were probably no more effective in curing smallpox and yellow fever than were those of the physicians. Usually, however, their treatments would do no further harm and might make the patient more comfortable. Colonial women were more willing than male physicians to borrow treatments from the Indians and black slaves. Women's "cookbooks," both the manuscript books kept by individuals and the printed books that might be purchased, contain recipes for medical remedies as well as for foods, including salves for sores, soothing syrups for sore throats, and even mixtures that it was fondly hoped would ward off such major killers as tuberculosis. Martha Washington, who had lost several relatives to that disease, prescribed "Capon Ale" as a cure. This was a combination of chicken soup and strong ale, surely more welcome to a dying patient than ipecac and leeches.

Opposite, left: **Bleeding Kit.** *Brass, pewter, steel, and wood, 1 × 9-1/2 × 16-1/2 in. Europe, c. 1780. Smithsonian Institution, Washington, D.C. (Photo: Ray Schwartz)*

Most people in colonial America relied on the treatments and herbal remedies offered by women. Although some women read medical textbooks, mothers usually passed favorite "receipts" on to their daughters. Like university-trained physicians, women favored bloodletting to remove the foul "humours" believed responsible for everything from sore throats to scarlet fever. Sharp-bladed contraptions called scarifiers were applied to the body of the patient, who sacrificed large quantities of precious blood on his dubious route to recovery.

Opposite, right: R. Havell, after George Walker, **Leech Finders.** *Hand-colored lithograph, 14 × 18 in. framed. London, 1814. Smithsonian Institution, Washington, D.C. (Photo: Ray Schwartz)*

The application of leeches was another bloodletting "cure" in pre-industrial America.

Right: Prudence Punderson, **The First, Second and Last Scene of Mortality.** *Crimped silk floss on satin, ink, 12-3/4 × 17 in. Preston, Connecticut, c. 1775. The Connecticut Historical Society, Hartford.*

Innumerable dangers worked to shorten the lifespan of the average 18th-century woman, and the young lady who summed up her life in this small needlework picture movingly expressed her acceptance of human frailty. Her vision of one woman's journey from the cradle to the grave is set within a single crowded room; only the central figure of the teen-aged Prudence (1758–84) separates the infant's cradle from the grim coffin. This touching portrayal of life's brevity was fulfilled in Prudence's case: she died less than ten years later at the age of 26.

The First, Second, and Last Scene of Mortality.   Prudence Punderson.

Gravestone Rubbing. *Grafton, Vermont. (Photo: Grafton Historical Society)*

This simple New England gravestone of 1803 is a poignant memorial to the sufferings of Rebecca Park – wife of Thomas K. Park – who died at the age of 40 and was buried with her son Thomas, Jr., and 13 other children in the family grave. On the left half of the stone shown here, the infants are portrayed as tiny death's-heads on the branches of a barren tree of life. The epitaph reads:

Youth behold and shed a tear
See fourteen children slumber here
See their image how they shine
Like flowers on a fruitful vine.

Behold and see as you pass by
My fourteen children with me lie
Old or young you soon must die
And turn to dust as well as I.

In Memory of
Thomas K. Park Jun.ʳ
and thirteen Infants.
Children of Mr.
Thomas K. Park and
Rebecca his wife.

Abby Bishop, **Sampler.** *Silk and wool on linen, 16-3/4 × 19 in. Providence, Rhode Island, 1796. Museum of Fine Arts, Boston. Gift of Mrs. Samuel Cabot.*

Daughter of Captain Lemuel Bishop of Providence, 13-year-old Abby (1783–1812) chose to portray the Providence Congregational Church when she embroidered this eulogy to her mother in 1796 at Miss Mary Balch's school. This sampler is believed to be the only dated American mourning embroidery of the 18th century.

Nathaniel Smibert (?), **Mrs. George Davies.** *Oil on canvas, 13 × 9-1/4 in. Massachusetts, c. 1750. Courtesy Massachusetts Historical Society, Boston.*

Extreme old age was considered a phenomenon during the 18th century when few Americans lived to reach their fifties. Certainly Mary Davies (or Davis) earned her reputation as a local curiosity before her death in 1752 at the age of 117, having outlived three husbands. Born Mary Mirick in Charlestown only fifteen years after the landing of the **Mayflower,** *she is believed to have had 9 children, 45 grandchildren, 215 great-grandchildren, and 800 great-great-grandchildren. The Reverend William Bentley of Salem recorded that "she could do a good day's work at shelling corn" at the age of 104 and still "sat at her spinning wheel" six years later.*

The odds against surviving to old age in early America were very great. But those who reached the age of sixty or seventy had to be such very strong physical specimens that it was not surprising for them to survive to their eighties, nineties, or even past the century mark. Those who lived to decline into feebleness or senility were cared for at home. Still, an extended family, in which elderly people lived with children, grandchildren, or great grandchildren, was extremely rare. Few people lived long enough to see their children grown, and fewer still to see their grandchildren.

In contrast to our age death came most frequently to the very young. There were few mothers who did not bury at least one child. Indeed, despite their large families, parents often left no surviving children. Diphtheria, yellow fever, or some nameless plague could easily carry off a dozen children in a few weeks. The reality of death could not be ignored or hidden. It was not something that happened just to old people hidden away in hospitals. On the contrary, it was often the most public event in an individual's life. Friends, neighbors, and relatives came to be present at a deathbed. It was a scene of great dignity in which the person about to expire had the central role. It was considered important to "die well," to speak last words that could be treasured by the witnesses, and to express last wishes that must be honored as sacred by survivors.

Although death was much in the minds of Americans of both the eighteenth and nineteenth centuries, a change in attitude began late in the eighteenth century. In the earlier years the attitude toward death was matter-of-fact. The list of friends, neighbors, and even family members who died was tucked into final paragraphs of letters without comment except, perhaps, an observation that one must bow to God's will. Tombstones were plain, ornamented only with such stark symbols as an hourglass or a death's head. Death was too familiar to romanticize, and deaths were too frequent to permit elaborate mourning. Toward the end of the eighteenth century, as both birth rate and death rate declined, mourning for individuals—especially the young—became more elaborate. Tombstones bore crude portraits of the deceased, and later angels, willow trees, and illustrations of weeping survivors became appropriate ornaments. It also became proper

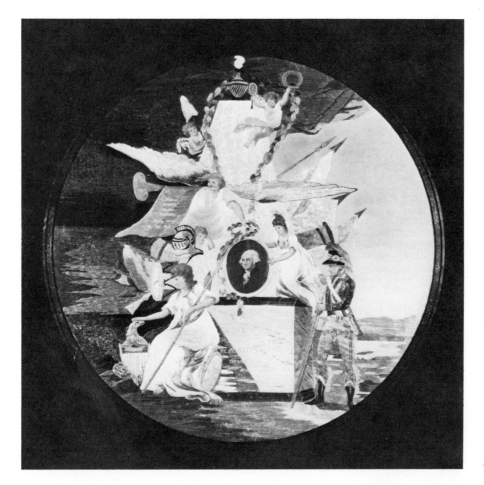

Anonymous, **Sacred to the Memory of Washington.** *Silk and watercolor on silk, 23 in. in diam. America, 1800–15. Mr. and Mrs. Gregg Ring.*

The death of George Washington on December 14, 1799, plunged the entire nation into mourning. In the pervasive mood of bereavement, early 19th-century schoolgirls produced a surprising number of silk embroidered mourning pictures, some dedicated to the memory of Washington and others eulogizing the death of loved ones. Although mourning jewelry bearing urns and willows was worn in America from the 1780s onward, the emergence of the composite needlework mourning picture — complete with inscribed tomb, willows, and weeping figure — seems to be tied to Washington's death. This allegorical embroidery is based on a contemporary Enoch Gridley engraving after the painting by John Coles, Jr., probably done in Boston c. 1800. Coles had borrowed a 1793 engraved portrait of Washington by Edward Savage to grace the center of his composition.

Mourning Brooch. *Watercolor on ivory, gold, pearls, glass, 2-1/2 × 1-5/8 × 3/6 in. England, 1780–85. The Colonial Williamsburg Foundation, Williamsburg, Va.*

Inscribed "Our darling Babe to Heaven has flown and left us in a World of pain, FCB April 3, 1780," this brooch was made in memory of Frances Courtenay Baylor, infant daughter of Colonel John Baylor and Frances Norton Baylor. The child was buried at the Baylor plantation at New Market, Carolina County, Virginia.

According to an old label on the reverse of the frame, this eloquent mourning picture was embroidered by the young lady shown kneeling at the tomb of her father, Shubael Abbe (1744–1804), a Yale graduate and the sheriff of Windham County.

to preserve reminders of the deceased in the home—not as they had been when they were alive, but as corpses. The portrait of Rachel Peale mourning over the body of her dead daughter anticipates the romantic attitude toward death that came to dominate in the nineteenth century. So do poems like one entitled "The Maiden" that were popular in the Victorian era:

> I saw a maiden young and fair,
> Laid on a snow-white bed;
> I should have deemed her sleeping there—
> But they told me, she was dead!

Women were central to the mourning practices of the nineteenth century. Both sexes were expected to have similar attitudes toward death in the eighteenth century, but nineteenth-century moralists believed that women were more sensitive, more pious, and generally closer to heaven than men. They became the chief mourners and the experts on the afterlife, which, after 1830, came to be popularly conceived as a "home beyond the skies," complete with kitchens, bedrooms, courtships, and concert performances, a domestic world particularly suited to Victorian women. The needlework mourning pictures produced in large numbers after 1799 offer the first evidence of these changing attitudes toward death.

Domesticity

The labor involved in keeping house in the pre-industrial era was considerable, and men were not insensible to the nature of their wives' work in providing the essential needs of the family. One gentleman wrote in 1778, "My wife's conduct verifies that old saying that 'woman's work is never done.'" Some months earlier he had made a long entry in his diary describing his wife's work around the house. "As I have, in this Memorandum," he wrote, "taken scarcely any notice of my wife's employment, it might appear as if her engagements were very trifling, the which is not the case but the reverse, and to do her that justice which her services deserve by entering them minutely would take up most of my time." Among the activities which he did take time to list, however, were "getting prepared in the kitchen, baking our own bread and pies, meat &c....cutting and drying apples...making of cider without tools...seeing all our washing done, and her fine clothes and my shirts, the which are all smoothed by her...her making of twenty large cheeses, and that from one cow, and daily using milk and cream, besides her sewing, knitting &c." The wife of Stephen Rogers merited notice in the local newspaper when, on a single day, she "milk'd 8 cows in the morning—made her cheeses—turned and took care of fourscore cheeses—made a number of beds—swept her house, consisting of three rooms—spun six skains of worsted yarn—baked a batch of bread—churned a quantity of butter—and milked 7 cows in the evening."

Cooking was a fundamental responsibility for all women, rich and poor. Wealthy families might dine elegantly on porcelain plates and enjoy elaborate meals prepared and served by numbers of servants supervised by the wife. In their homes functional cooking equipment was supplemented by such items as nutmeg graters and larding pins made of silver that were intended purely for show. Most middle-class families dined much more simply and were pleased to have pewter dishes and spoons and a bit of fresh meat or cheese to eat with their bread and ale. Many families had only wooden trenchers and ate with their fingers the monotonous diet of corn mush, salt meat, and grog, cider, or molasses beer. The poor diet of Americans made scurvy a constant threat throughout the colonial period.

Fresh vegetables, fruit, and a few flowers might be provided by a woman's kitchen garden. But even when fresh vegetables were served, they were boiled for hours beforehand and so lost their vitamin content. The slaves, who cooked for themselves in their huts, also overcooked their vegetables; but they prized the "pot likker" and so did not lose all nutritional benefits. Maintaining the kitchen garden and overseeing livestock were important agricultural activities of white women. The native American women were often in charge of all the agricultural work of their tribes. Their work was basic to the Indian diet, for the native Americans ate much less meat than the white population and their crops provided most of their food. With few exceptions, the Indian tribes ate very well. Indian women understood the need to balance diets and prepared meats, vegetables, fish, nuts, and fruit. They dried berries for use in the wintertime, thus avoiding scurvy. The native American women had some surprisingly sophisticated recipes—including the original baked beans and clam bakes. Black women, too, had their own methods of preparing the food available to them, many of which are the basis for the famous "southern cooking" style.

Frontispiece engraving from E. Smith, **Compleat Housewife: or Accomplish'd Gentlewoman's Companion. Being a Collection of upwards of Six Hundred of the most approved Receipts in Cookery ... To which is added A Collection of above Three Hundred Family Receipts of Medicines: viz. Drinks, Syrups, Salves, Ointments, and various other things of sovereign and approved Efficacy in most Distempers, Pains, Aches, Wounds, Sores, &c.** *8 × 5-1/4 in. 14th ed. London, 1750. The Library Company of Philadelphia. (Photo: Joseph Kelley)*

Blacks and Indians developed cooking into an art, but most colonial families existed on a simple unappetizing diet that varied little from day to day. Indeed it was only the very wealthy with surplus food, many servants, and lavish dining equipment who bothered to prepare interesting menus. It was these women who turned to printed cookbooks to plan meals in imitation of the European gentry. Although some women kept handwritten books of "receipts," printed cookbooks were not widely used by colonial women.

A Selection of 18th-century Cooking Tools.
Colonial Williamsburg Foundation,
Williamsburg, Va. (Photo: Peggy Barnett)

Left: Kitchen Equipment. Old Salem,
Inc., Winston-Salem, N. C. (Photo: Peggy
Barnett)

In addition to preparing food, colonial women were responsible for manufacturing a variety of items needed in the home, such as candles and soap. Indian women produced baskets, cradleboards, and also built and moved the tepees or longhouses. The most important items manufactured by women, however, were clothing and bedcoverings.

Spinning, weaving, sewing, knitting, and quilting were constant occupations for the white colonists. White women who came to live with the Indians were glad to find they were relieved of these chores in native American society. Compared to the Europeans, most of the Indians wore little clothing—they depended on layers of grease to protect them from the weather. Most of what they wore was for ornament only. The exception was moccasins, and, in northern areas, snowshoes, both of which were produced by women. Indian clothes made from animal skins and furs were far easier to produce than woven cloth garments.

The need of white Americans for clothing, both for modesty and warmth, made great demands on women in the pre-industrial age when ready-made fabrics were too expensive for ordinary people to afford. Although both boys and girls were taught the rudiments of sewing and mending and some men worked as professional weavers to prepare cloth from yarn spun by women in their homes, women in rural areas usually had to manufacture their families' clothing without assistance. This was a time-consuming, never-ending task. Since it took nearly a year and a half to create linen from flax, a man's shirt often wore out by the time a woman could complete a new one.

Most women were not skilled tailors. While a wealthy family might hire a dressmaker to cut and sew fabric, most women made clothing that was loosely cut and bore little resemblance to the elegant silk and satin gowns depicted in colonial portraits or preserved in museums. Many women owned only one dress at any given time in their lives, and some women wore the same dress for several decades. Clothing was mended, cut down, restyled, and finally cut up for rags or bedcoverings. Consequently, very little everyday clothing from the pre-industrial period has survived. The dress of a typical colonial woman consisted of a coarse linen or cotton chemise covered by a bodice of homespun cloth or leather that was loosely cut and sometimes laced in front. The chemise was the basic article of underclothing worn by women of all classes until well into the nineteenth century; for most women in Revolutionary America, it was the only undergarment, for women apparently did not wear drawers, and more fashionable underpinnings, such as stays and panniers, were worn by only a few. Chemises were both long and short, and elegant varieties were made of fine linen often with ruffled trim at the neck and sleeves. Skirts were full and fell only to the ankle. For added warmth, a woman might wear two or three petticoats under a wool skirt, or she might wear a petticoat alone without a skirt.

Opposite above: The Garden at Wicks House, Morristown, New Jersey. (Photo: Peggy Barnett)

Few colonial Americans maintained elegant formal gardens near their homes, but women usually kept small vegetable and herb gardens to stock the kitchen larder and to provide ingredients for medicinal remedies.

Opposite, below: Advertisement from the **South Carolina Gazette,** *March 14, 1768. Charleston Library Society, Charleston, S.C. (Photo: Louis Schwartz)*

Contemporary almanacs and newspapers frequently carried gardening hints or notices of new seeds, and some people owned copies of specialized manuals, such as Philip Miller's **Gardener's Dictionary.** *Martha Daniell Logan (1704–79), a South Carolina schoolteacher and noted horticulturalist, offered gardening tips in her* **Gardener's Kalendar,** *which first appeared in John Tobler's* **South Carolina Almanack** *in 1752 and continued intermittently until the 1780s. It was succeeded by the expanded* **Gardener's Calendar,** *published posthumously under her name in the* **Palladium of Knowledge** *from 1796 to 1804 (with breaks). She also sold seeds and roots from her home in Charleston and carried on a lively correspondence with the Pennsylvania botanist John Bartram, whom she met in 1760.*

Right: Washtubs. Old Salem, Inc., Winston-Salem, N.C. (Photo: Peggy Barnett)

Cherokee Basket. *Cane, 4-3/4 × 7-1/2 ×
6 in. Cherokee, c. 1730–80. Courtesy Peabody
Museum of Archaeology and Ethnology,
Cambridge, Mass. (Photo: Hillel Burger)*
Cherokee women used cane baskets of this type
for general housework.

Below: **Chemise.** *Linen. Massachusetts,
1800–10. Courtesy Society for the
Preservation of New England Antiquities,
Boston. (Photo: Richard Cheek)*

Opposite, above: **Short Cotton Gown and
Silk Petticoat.** *Pennsylvania, 1790–1810
(gown), 1740–80 (petticoat). Chester County
Historical Society, West Chester, Pa. (Photo:
Peggy Barnett)*

*This short gown, made from an English
printed cotton, belonged to Thomazine
Downing Thomas, whose husband was a
colonel in the Revolutionary War and a
member of Congress. It is shown with an
earlier silk petticoat made by the Pennsylvania
needlework teacher Ann Marsh (1717–97).*

Opposite, below: **Open Robe.** *Block-printed
linen. Pennsylvania, 1730–60. Chester
County Historical Society, West Chester, Pa.
(Photo: Peggy Barnett)*

*This rare example of everyday clothing is
shown with a silk petticoat of the 19th century.*

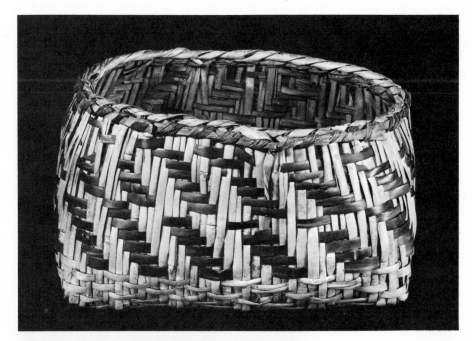

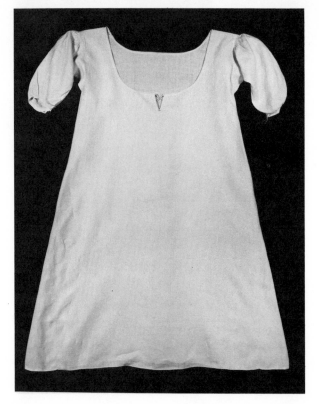

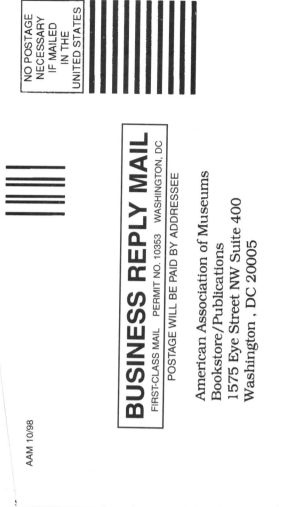

...sisted of a simple home-
...ns were able to purchase
...titched in a scaled-down
...so wore short blouses or
...over a skirt or petticoat.
...n stockings, a homespun
...utdoor wear. Shoes were
...ne areas moccasins were
...refoot.

...verings were as essential
...cessories were often the
...n the home. Once settle-
...warm and colorful "bed
...ed ruggs, long known in
...the surface made flat or
...ury many women embel-
...orked in floral patterns.
...eteenth century but was
...ury, was, essentially, any
...ogether. Quilts not only
...but were also an econom-
...aps of fabric. Although
...with them from England,
few examples made before 1775 exist today.

Some quilt tops were pieced from small bits of fabric or made by appliqué-
ing patterned cutouts to a basic ground material. Once the top layer was completed, it was placed on a large, rectangular frame for the actual quilting or
stitching together of both sides, an affair that developed into the popular "quilting bee" of the nineteenth century. As with clothing, the bedcoverings of
ordinary people rarely survived. Only relatively wealthy women could spare
the time to ornament such utilitarian items, but those who did raised the production of bedcovers to a highly developed art form.

Colonial women obviously took great pride in their needlework, often
their only creative outlet. Mrs. Elizabeth Wyche of Virginia chose to have her
portrait painted while she was engaged with her needle and thread, and elegant sewing accessories, such as silver and gold sewing chatelaines and thimbles,
were treasured possessions. Even highly intelligent and well-educated women

Opposite: **Blanket.** *Woolen crewels on wool, 96 × 80 in. America, c. 1770. Greenfield Village and Henry Ford Museum, Dearborn, Mich.*

Above, right: Woodcut from **Mother Goose's Melody: or Sonnets for the Cradle.** *4 × 2-5/8 in. Worcester, Massachusetts, Isaiah Thomas, 1794. American Antiquarian Society, Worcester, Mass.*

Below right: Esther Wheat, **Quilt.** *Indigo wool, wool filling, tan wool lining (red wool lining added later), 91 × 93 in. Conway, Massachusetts, c. 1790. Smithsonian Institution, Washington, D.C.*

Many of the early surviving American quilts are whole cloth spreads stitched in a variety of intricate patterns like the glazed wool example shown here.

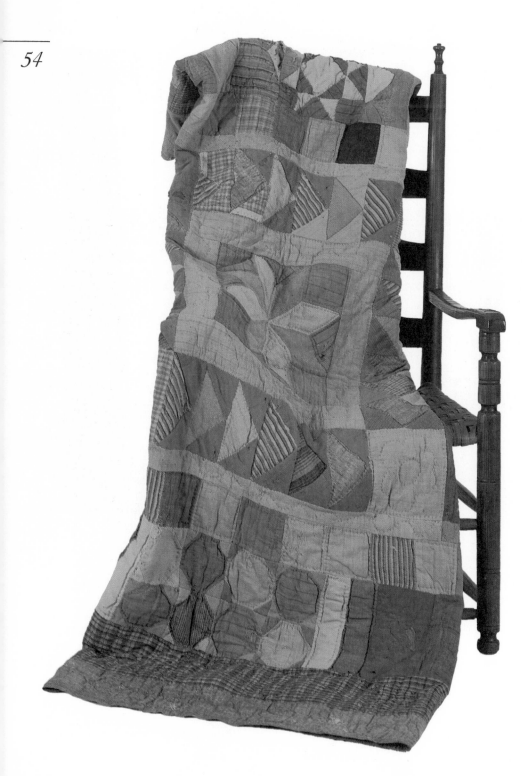

Left: **Pieced Quilt.** *Homespun linen and wool fillings, 76-1/2 × 62-1/2 in. America, 1790–1820. Museum of Early Southern Decorative Arts, Winston-Salem, N.C. (Photo: Bradford Rauschenberg)*

Although the unknown workers who pieced this quilt made an elementary attempt at design, their main concern was warmth. The surfaces of pieced homespun rags are thickly padded and rather haphazardly sewed together; some areas are unquilted, while others are tacked down in simple semicircles and squares. Several sections of the quilt top are appliquéd, using a basting stitch, with rough edges floating on the surface. Although it reflects neither artistic talent nor skilled needlework, the quilt is a valuable record of a common, utilitarian type of covering found on most early American beds.

Above: **Bed Rugg.** *Wool with embroidered wool knots, 84-1/2 × 66 in. Virginia, 1770–1800. Association for the Preservation of Virginia Antiquities, Richmond. (Photo courtesy of The Magazine Antiques)*

Unlike other bed coverings that might incorporate ready-made fabrics, "bed ruggs" were entirely of home manufacture, with the designs and colors worked out well in advance. Although they bear a resemblance to hooked rugs, the techniques used were those of knotting and embroidery onto a homespun foundation surface. Most surviving bed ruggs were made in New England during the 18th century, though contemporary records indicate use in other colonies. This rare knotted southern example shares design elements with contemporary East Indian cottons printed or painted with a central "tree of life" motif.

Above, right: Bedroom of the innkeeper and his wife in the 1784 Salem Tavern. Old Salem, Inc. Winston-Salem, N.C. (Photo: Peggy Barnett)

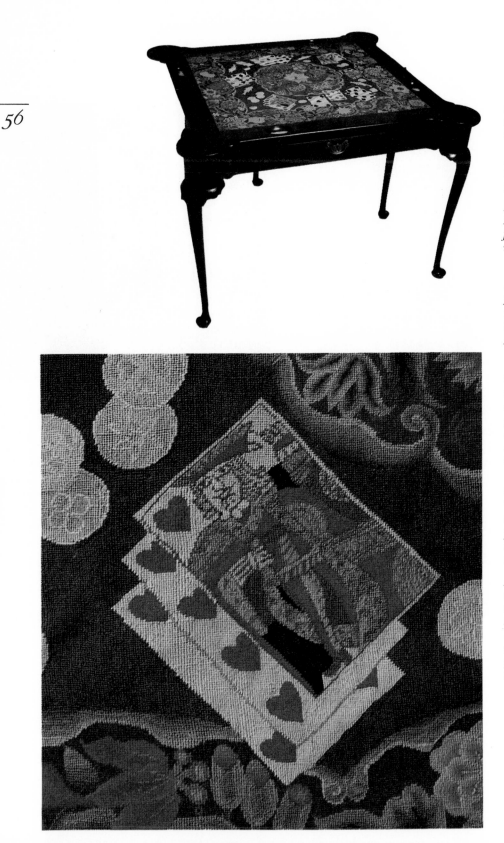

Left: **Card Table.** *Mahogany with pine and maple, wool embroidered top worked by Mercy Otis Warren, 27-1/4 × 41-1/8 × 38-1/2 in. Boston (table) and Plymouth, Massachusetts, 1750–70. The Pilgrim Society, Plymouth, Mass. (Photo: Peggy Barnett)*

Like other accomplished ladies of her day, Mercy Otis Warren was skilled in the art of fancy embroidery, as seen in the detail reproduced below.

Opposite left: Cephas Thompson (attrib.), **Elizabeth Wyche** *(?). Oil on canvas, 31-1/2 × 21-1/2 in. Virginia, 1800–10. Mrs. John Van B. Metts. (Photo: Bradford Rauschenberg)*

Opposite, right: **Chatelaine with Sewing Tools.** *Silver chatelaine, 26 in.; steel scissors, 4-1/2 in.; pincushion silk on canvas, 2-1/4 in. Pennsylvania, 1799. Chester County Historical Society, West Chester, Pa. (Photo: Peggy Barnett)*

Opposite, below: **Work Table.** *Mahogany and bird's-eye maple with painted decoration; secondary wood, pine, 28-1/4 × 20-1/2 × 15-1/4 in. Portland, Maine (?), c. 1810. Museum of Fine Arts, Boston.*

Although needlework was a necessary skill as well as an accomplishment for 18th-century women, specialized furniture to hold tools and sewing were not available in America until the 1790s. Before that time women stored their work and tools wherever they could, usually in pockets worn under the skirt or in portable woven baskets.

Far left: **Hunting Pouch.** *Beaded cloth, 9 × 7-3/4 in. Cherokee, 1790–1820. Courtesy Peabody Museum of Archaeology and Ethnology, Cambridge, Mass. (Photo: Hillel Burger)*

Southeastern beadwork is rare.

Left: **Black pouch Thunderbird.** *Leather with porcupine quill ornament, 8-3/4 × 6 in. Iroquois, c. 1750. Peabody Museum of Archaeology and Ethnology, Cambridge, Mass.*

Opposite, above:
Pocketbook. *Wool in Irish stitch on canvas, silk, 4-3/8 × 6-1/2 in. Pennsylvania, 1776. Chester County Historical Society, West Chester, Pa. (Photo: Peggy Barnett)*

Opposite, center:
Ann Marsh (attrib.), **Seat Cushion.** *Silk and wool on canvas, 18-1/2 × 21-3/4 in. Pennsylvania, 1740–80. Chester County Historical Society, West Chester, Pa. (Photo: Peggy Barnett)*

Opposite, below:
Pockets. *Wool on canvas, 13 × 10 in. Pennsylvania, 1740–90. Chester County Historical Society, West Chester, Pa. (Photo: Peggy Barnett)*

These baggy carry-alls were usually made of plain linen, dimity, or pieced scraps of leftover fabrics, while others were elaborate creations in crewel, or – as in this case – brilliant Irish-stitch embroidery. A French visitor to Delaware in 1796 wrote that it was "terrible in a lady to wear a pair of **pockets** *– the French ladies never did such a thing."*

turned to complex needlework projects for occupation and stimulation. In advising his daughter Martha to learn fine embroidery, Thomas Jefferson wrote in 1787: "In the country life of America there are many moments when a woman can have recourse to nothing but her needle for employment." Such busy and important women as Martha Washington, Mercy Otis Warren, and Abigail Adams had a lifelong interest in fine needlework. Often these projects involved the decoration of practical household effects, and few articles were spared. Potholders, belts, seat cushions, and pocketbooks all received the attentions of talented embroiderers during the eighteenth and nineteenth centuries.

Indian women also developed art forms in which decoration of functional items was raised far above the level of craft. Beadwork and porcupine-quill embroidery were the oldest and most widely practiced of native American embroidery techniques, although there were many other forms, including some employing feathers, fish skins, and appliqué in furs. An oral tradition preserved among the northern tribes describes artistic talent as a special gift of the Great Spirit, Saghalee Tyee, to the first woman. "She [the first woman] was asleep and dreaming of her ignorance of how to please man, and she prayed to Saghalee Tyee to help her. He breathed on her and gave her something that she couldn't see, or hear, or smell, or touch, and it was preserved in a little basket, and by it all the arts of design and skilled handiwork were imparted to her descendants." In some tribes a deity known as Spider Woman was identified as the founder of all needle arts, and special symbolic designs were said to come from her to women in dreams. Indian and white women appreciated the skill of each other's work, and their designs sometimes reflected the influence of one another's traditions.

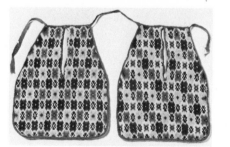

Women at Work

Priscilla Abbot, at her Shop. *Receipt printed and completed in manuscript, 7-9/32 × 4-17/32 in. Salem, Mass., April 19, 1794. Courtesy Massachusetts Historical Society, Boston. (Photo: George M. Cushing)*

Opposite: The Margaret Hunter Millinery Shop (reconstruction). Colonial Williamsburg Foundation, Williamsburg, Va. (Photo: Peggy Barnett)

There was such a great shortage of labor in the pre-industrial age that there was no such thing as a leisure class. Before the Revolution even wealthy ladies and gentlemen had work to do. Wealthy women did much of their own housework, and the duties of overseeing a large family, which included numerous servants and slaves, made the mistress of a wealthy home a combination of housekeeper, factory overseer, and community midwife. Only after the shortage of labor eased and some families were able to accumulate great fortunes could a leisure class of ladies devoted to ornamental rather than practical occupations develop.

The occupation of most American families from the wealthiest to the poorest was farming. Ordinarily husbands and wives worked together to assure that the family would be self-sufficient and, it was hoped, make a profit. Women who were widowed, however, or those husbands were away—as a great many were during the Revolution—ran their farms by themselves. Most colonial women had sons or male servants or slaves to do the actual field work. White women did not usually labor in the fields, but those desperate to survive could not be fussy about the work they did, and when necessary poor farm women would plow and harvest. Women were often quite successful in their independent farming ventures. The best-known of the women who made fortunes in agriculture was the capable Eliza Lucas Pinckney, who, at the age of twenty-one, while running her father's South Carolina plantation, successfully introduced the cultivation of indigo to the colony. Indigo, a blue dye, was a leading source of South Carolina's prosperity in the years before the American Revolution. After experimenting for several years, Eliza Lucas produced her first successful indigo crop in 1744. She distributed seed from this crop to other planters, and in 1747 South Carolina exported almost one hundred thousand pounds of indigo to England. Since cloth manufacture was England's chief industry, and dye was an essential part of the manufacturing process, the English were delighted to have one of their colonies become a source for indigo, which they would otherwise have had to buy from colonies belonging to their French enemies. Parliament voted to grant a bounty to planters producing indigo, so that the South Carolina planters had a valuable supplement to their rice crop until the Revolution ended this profitable arrangement. Eliza Pinckney was interested in agriculture throughout her life. After her husband's death she ran the seven plantations that he had owned and continued to experiment with improved methods of cultivation.

The full participation of the farmer's wife in the family business has been the rule throughout American history into modern times. In the eighteenth century, however, women were productively employed in all of the occupations entered by men, since all occupations centered in the home or a nearby office or workshop, and women and children as well as men worked to make a success of the family enterprise. There was no formal licensing required for the practice of law and medicine until the end of the eighteenth century, so that women might draft wills and other legal documents. Some appeared in court arguing on their own behalf or as attorney for an absent husband. As we have seen, women monopolized obstetrical practice until the last part of the century, and they were preferred as medical practitioners by most of the population. Only after schools of law and medicine were established were women driven from the practice of these professions.

The Margaret Hunter Millinery Shop (reconstruction). Colonial Williamsburg Foundation, Williamsburg, Va. (Photo: Peggy Barnett)

Opposite, above:

Eliza Lucas Pinckney, **Letter to "My Dear Child."** *10-1/4 × 8 in. South Carolina, September 10, 1785. Charleston Library Society, S.C.*

In response to an inquiry from one of her children, Eliza Pinckney (1722?–1793) here recounts the methods she used to pioneer the successful cultivation of indigo in South Carolina.

Opposite, below:

From the **Boston News-Letter,** *September 4, 1755. The New York Public Library.*

All the crafts and trades practiced in early America included at least a few women. Most women worked in an enterprise controlled by a husband or father, but widows and spinsters had to carry on alone. Colonial newspapers printed advertisements of women in every business, from those of apothecary and blacksmith to shipwright and undertaker. Widow Mankin of Philadelphia sold to the public "such things as are principally used in the Modern Practice of Physick, being a great variety of Materia Medica, both simple and compound, Cymical and Gallenical." Mary Salmon of Boston ran a shop "where all gentlemen may have their Horses shod in the best Manner, as also all sorts of Blacksmith's Work done with Fidelity and Dispatch." In New York City Marguerite Hastier was a silversmith, and a Mrs. Sommer ground glass for spectacles. Jane Massey of Charleston, South Carolina, was a gunsmith, and Mary Wilson of Norfolk, Virginia, was a shoemaker. Elizabeth Russell advertised as a shipwright in the *South Carolina Gazette,* and Lydia Darragh told the readers of the *Pennsylvania Gazette* that she would "make Grave-Clothes, and lay out the Dead, in the neatest Manner."

Such newspaper advertisements reflect a society in which there was much economic opportunity for women and in which women eagerly sought out business possibilities. For instance, the *Virginia Gazette* of November 17, 1752, carried an advertisement placed by Mr. and Mrs. John Walker of Williamsburg. The husband offered to instruct young men in reading, writing, arithmetic, the classics, geography, and history, while his wife proposed to teach young women "all Kinds of Needle Work" and to make "Capuchins, Shades, Hats, and Bonnets." In 1776 a mother and daughter took a joint ad in which the mother announced her intention to practice as a midwife while the daughter ran a boarding school for girls where reading, writing, arithmetic, French, and needlework would be taught. In 1787 an extremely enterprising woman in North Carolina placed an advertisement in which she offered to do any kind of needlework and to teach needlework, to clean teeth, implant false teeth, treat "the Fever and Ague" by means of her own "speedy and infallible remedy," and to cure "all the diseases of the Eyes." Apparently there had been some question of her proficiency in such a wide variety of trades since she concluded her advertisement by saying, "She flatters herself the discerning public will pay no kind of attention, to any malicious reports her enemies may circulate to her disadvantage."

Women who kept shops might sell products they made themselves, and some were import merchants who stocked goods from abroad. Other women sold foodstuffs or small items as street venders. A substantial proportion of the printers and newspaper publishers of colonial America were women. Since women were established in the printing industry in England, France, Germany, and Holland during the seventeenth century, it is not surprising that the tradition should continue in America. During the colonial period six women served as official printers to provincial governments, and one of them, Anne Catherine Hoof Green, was the public printer for the city of Annapolis from 1767 to 1775. Sarah Updike Goddard, who published the *Providence Gazette,* taught the trade to her children, and her daughter, Mary Katharine Goddard, published the *Maryland Journal and Baltimore Advertiser.* Women printers produced almanacs and books as well as newspapers and might take on other work as a

early fond of the vegetable world, my Father was plea[sed]
with it and encouraged it, he told me the turn I
had for those amusements might produce something
of real and public utility, if I could bring to perfection
the plants of other countries which he would procure
me: accordingly when he went to the west Indies
he sent me a variety of seeds, among them the
Indigo, I was ignorant both of the proper season for
sowing it, and the soil best adapted to it. to the
best of my recollection I first try'd it in March
1741, or 1742. It was destroyed (I think by a frost)
The next time in April, and it was cut down
by a worm; I persevered to a third planting and
succeeded, and when I informed my Father it be[came]

Life, Laſt Words and Dying CONFESSION,

O F

RACHEL WALL,

Who, with *William Smith* and *William Dunogan*, were executed at Boston, on Thursday, October 8, 1789, for
HIGH-WAY ROBBERY.

Left: Benjamin Henry Latrobe,
Nondescripts attracted by a neighbouring barbecue, near the Oaks, Virginia. *Pencil and ink wash, 6-15/16 × 10-15/16 in. Virginia, 1796. Papers of Benjamin Henry Latrobe, Maryland Historical Society, Baltimore.*

In colonial America children were put to work as early as possible, usually in their own homes. Some poor girls were apprenticed as servants to learn a trade, while others took to the street to peddle matches, coal, and trinkets. This sketch shows a group of peddlers on their way to a country barbecue to sell peaches.

Below, left: **Life, Last Words and Dying Confession of Rachel Wall.** *Broadside, 17-1/2 × 13-9/16 in. Boston, 1789. Courtesy Massachusetts Historical Society, Boston. (Photo: George M. Cushing)*

Opposite, above: **The Maryland, Delaware, Pennsylvania, Virginia, and North-Carolina Almanack, and Ephemeris....** *Printed by M. K. Goddard, Baltimore, 1781. Library of the Maryland Historical Society, Baltimore.*

Opposite, below: Anonymous, **Mary Katharine Goddard.** *Engraving after a lost portrait printed in Joseph Towne Wheeler,* **The Maryland Press, 1777–1790.** *(Photo: Library of the Maryland Historical Society)*

Daughter of the Rhode Island printer Sarah (Updike) Goddard, Mary Katharine Goddard (1738–1816) was herself a printer, newspaper publisher, the postmaster of Baltimore, and a bookseller. She assisted her mother in publishing the **Providence Gazette** *and later assisted her brother on the* **Pennsylvania Chronicle** *and the* **Maryland Journal.**

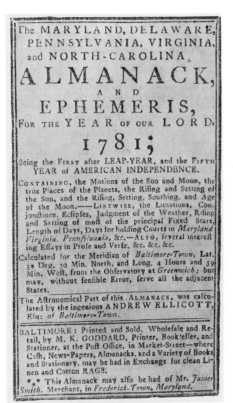

sideline. Eliza Anderson Godefroy of Baltimore, for instance, did translations while producing a literary journal, *The Observer*, which she edited under the pseudonym of Beatrice Ironside, and other women were known as bookbinders or stationers.

Some women spurned honest occupations and attempted to support themselves by a life of crime. A Maryland newspaper reported on March 20, 1755, that "Penelope House, was twice whipp'd, and twice stood in the Pillory, for Shop-lifting." A broadside dated 1789 contained a lengthy history of Rachel Wall, who confessed herself guilty of "almost every...sin a person could commit, except murder." She and two male accomplices were executed for highway robbery.

In the nineteenth century, as the center of economic activity moved away from the home into factories and offices, most occupations came to be viewed as unsuitable for women or incompatible with their work in the home. The few jobs that remained open to them came to be typed as "women's" jobs, and most middle-class and upper-class women withdrew from the work force. Those of the middle class who did leave their homes to work were mostly young girls who had no interest in training themselves for skilled work since they expected to retire from the labor force when they married. As the American population grew and the labor shortage eased, the economic opportunities for women narrowed even further. They were no longer regarded as skilled workers in all trades and crafts, but were considered easily replaceable unskilled workers. As factories became established, women were grouped in the lowest-paying, least-skilled jobs, and by the early nineteenth century it was accepted practice to pay women much less than men for comparable work.

In the pre-industrial period in America, men and women earned equal pay. Tobacco and corn cost as much when purchased from a woman farmer as when purchased from a man, and it cost as much to have a female blacksmith shoe a horse as it cost to have a man do the work. Women who were printers or sextons received remuneration equal to that of males, and servants and slaves of both sexes received comparable allowances of food and clothing. Technically, of course, most women who worked in the eighteenth century, even those who made the most money, can be said to have worked actually for no more than room and board. For while women got equal wages or made equal profits, the law did not recognize their right to control this income. But most husbands did not exploit their rights to their women's earnings, and usually allowed them great freedom and provided for them lavishly when they could afford to do so. Still, the right of a husband to his wife's property was exercised frequently enough to make it clear that the right was not a dead letter by any means.

Widows and spinsters could hold property of their own, but it was difficult to make a living outside of a family business in the eighteenth century, and unmarried women were often impoverished. Some of the early textile factories were set up to give employment to such "deserving poor." An advertisement in a Pennsylvania newspaper in 1775 was addressed: "To the SPINNERS in this CITY and the SUBURBS. Your services are now wanted to promote the American Manufactory.... One distinguishing characteristic of an excellent woman as given by the wisest of men is, 'that she seeketh Wool and Flax, and worketh willingly with her hands....' In this time of public distress you have each of you an opportunity not only to help to sustain your families, but likewise to cast your mite into the treasury of the public good."

Most unattached women, however, worked as servants. Some might work for their keep by spinning and doing other household tasks in the home of a relative, while others worked for room and board and possibly a small wage in the home of strangers. Eighteenth-century newspapers show that women were employed as wet nurses, dairymaids, governesses, cooks, and even slave overseers. Servants who accepted positions such as these had a certain amount of independence; even though their wages might be low, they were free to resign the position to take another or to marry. Many servants, however, were bound by contracts called indentures, which left them with little more freedom than slaves.

Indentured servants, like slaves, were sold at auction to the highest bidder. Sometimes these people had sold themselves voluntarily to shipmasters in Europe in return for their passage to America, where they hoped that eventually they would be free and make a better life for themselves than was possible at home. Others were transported to America as servants as punishment for crime. And a good many were kidnapped or tricked into boarding cramped ships that carried them across the sea to labor in a strange land. In 1767 Alexander Stewart advertised "Just Imported, in the Ship Thornton, Christopher Reed, Master, ONE HUNDRED and FIFTY-TWO Seven Years Servants, among whom are great Variety of Tradesmen and Farmers, several Boys, and many notable Women." In 1773 a sale at the county wharf in Baltimore featured "A number of healthy indentured servants from London, among whom are the following, viz. a Clock and Watchmaker, a Smith and Farrier, a Shoemaker, a Basketmaker... several Husbandmen, Housemaids, Needlewomen, and a very good Milliner." All of these people worked without pay for the term of their indenture for whoever purchased them. If they did not like the work or their owner, they could not quit; they must run away. The owner would then advertise for their return, just as in the case of slaves. Among those advertised for in the *Pennsylvania Gazette* during the year 1776 were "an Irish servant Girl, named Catharine Lindon, much pock-marked, a thick chunky girl, with her hair tied, and it is almost black; she is supposed to be with child; had on, and took with her, one petticoat, with red, black, and white stripes, one fine shift, one bed sheet, one white linen bed gown, one striped ditto, half-worn shoes, and perhaps other clothes that are not yet missed." Her owner offered a twenty-shilling reward.

Opposite, above:

Anonymous, **The Fortunate Transport. Rob Theif: or the Lady of ye Gold Watch Polly Haycock.** *Engraving, 11-1/4 × 15-3/4 in. England, 1760–80. Colonial Williamsburg Foundation, Williamsburg, Va.*

Many unmarried women came to America during the colonial period in the hope of finding a man who would pay their passage and then marry them. Unlucky women were sold as indentured servants, so that they could pay off their debts by laboring for a specified period. Masters sometimes sold their servants just as they did their slaves, and while many were kind and considerate, others beat and cruelly abused these women.

Indentured women were not allowed to marry without their master's permission, and elopements were punished by whippings and increased periods of servitude. This unusual engraving chronicles the adventures of a young Englishwoman who sailed to America after having a bastard child, and was "whipped during Dinner her Master boasting that no Monarch on Earth had so fine Musick as he fancied her Cries." Rescued and wed to a local Justice, she ended her adventure as the wealthy mistress of a plantation, beating her own servants, "tho She felt the Misery herself."

Opposite, below:

John Greenwood, **Jersey Nanny** *(Ann Arnold). Mezzotint, 11 × 9 in. Boston, Massachusetts, J. Turner, 1748. Museum of Fine Arts, Boston. Gift of Henry L. Shattuck.*

In the late 1740s the artist engraved this portrait of the "common Mother," a swarthy-faced domestic wearing coarse homespun clothing held together with pins. Stressing the humanity of all people regardless of race or class, Greenwood added a barbed reminder to the pale and elegant ladies of Boston:

*Nature her various Skill displays
In thousand Shapes, a thousand Ways;
Tho' one Form differs from another
She's still of all the common Mother;
Then Ladies, let not Pride resist her,
But own that NANNY is your sister.*

Above: From the Essex (Massachusetts) Gazette, February 25–March 3, 1772. New York Public Library.

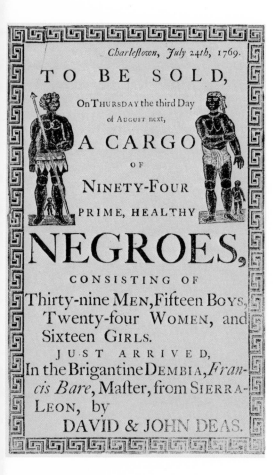

To be Sold...A Cargo of Ninety-Four Prime, Healthy Negroes. Broadside, 12-1/2 × 7-3/4 in. Charleston, South Carolina, 1769. American Antiquarian Society, Worcester, Mass.

Another Irish runaway was Jane Shepherd, described as "about 5 feet 3 inches high, of a fair complexion, pretty fat and lusty, has black hair, and is about 23 years of age...she inclines much to smoking of tobacco, and her under jaw teeth are black." A reward of three pounds was offered for Margaret Collins, "aged above 30 years, remarkably large, fond of company and drink, and very impertinent and talkative when in liquor." Poor children might be put into indentures as apprentices, and one sometimes reads of little girls as young as eight or nine who are advertised as runaways suspected of having gone to their parents.

Indentured servants served for limited periods of time. Although they owed absolute obedience to their owners during their term of service, the indenture also guaranteed them certain rights. The indenture of Ann Christine Fielthisen, for example, was to run for eight years and included her purchaser's promise to provide "sufficient Meat, Drink, Apparel, Washing and Lodging" and also to teach her to read the Bible and give her "two Compleat suits of apparel one whereof to be new" when her term expired. Thirteen-year-old Catherine Potts was to get her keep for the term of five years and also "to be taught the art and mystery of Housewifery," have "five quarters half-day schooling," and twenty dollars in cash as well as two sets of clothing when her time was up. A servant could sue in court to enforce these rights, as well as to protest any cruelty by the master.

Black slaves had none of these protections. They had no choice whatever in the conditions under which they came to America, and they had to serve for life, with their children following them into a condition of lifelong servitude. Both women and men were usually put to hard labor in the fields, and by the end of the eighteenth century black women were almost never trained in a craft by which they might hope to support themselves if they ran away. Spinning was virtually the only alternative to labor in the fields except for a few privileged house servants, and generally only the old and sick were allowed to spin. George Washington's diaries record some of the work assigned to his black women: October 27, 1787, "At the Ferry set 3 plows to Work—put the girl Eby to one of them." May 5, 1787, "The Women Preparing, and hoeing the New grd. in front of the House." April 11, 1787, "The Women...were hoeing the Wet part of the grd. between the Meadows which the plows could not touch. Ordered them as soon as this was done to go to the Ferry, and Assist in getting the grd. in the New Meadow in order for Oats and Timothy." January 21, 1788, "...two Men were cutting Trunnels for Fences, and the Women were carrying Rails from the swamp side to the Division fence." Such women clearly worked harder for smaller rewards than any other group in American society.

Published August 16, 1754 Pursuant to the Statute the Eighth of George the Second.

ELIZABETH CANNING,

Drawn from the Life, as fhe ftood at the Bar to receive her Sentence, in the Seffion's-Houfe, in the *Old-Bailey*.

THIS unfortunate young Girl was indicted for wilful and corrupt Perjury, for fwearing againft *Mary Squires*, commonly called the OLD GYPSEY, and her Evidence ftrongly corroborated by VIRTUE HALL, a Woman that liv'd with Mrs. *Sufannah Wells*, that kept a Houfe of Ill Fame at *Endfield Wafh*, where *Canning* fwore fhe was rob'd by the GYPSEY, and confin'd twenty-eight Days. Upon the Evidence of thefe two Parties, the GYPSEY was capitally convicted, and receiv'd Sentence of Death accordingly, and Mrs. *Wells* burned in the Hand, with fix Months Imprifonment, for concealing the Felon after the Felony was committed. Soon after that abandon'd Wretch *Virtue Hall* recanted, and faid, that what fhe had fworn againft the GYPSEY, was intirely falfe, and that fhe never faw ELIZABETH CANNING till the Time fhe was brought down by fome Gentlemen to furvey Mrs. *Well*'s Houfe. This Recantation occafion'd a ftrict Enquiry into this myfterious Affair.

Upon that Enquiry a Bill was preferr'd, and found to be a true Bill by the Grand Jury on that Head. Some of her Friends entered into a Recognizance of a large Sum, that fhe fhould appear, and take her Tryal at the Seffions following: Accordingly on the firft Day of *May* 1754 fhe was furrender'd, and appear'd at the Bar, and was arraign'd; and immediately the Court proceeded to Tryal, which lafted that Day, and the fix fucceffive Days following. When the Tryal was over, the Recorder of *London* repeated the Evidence on both Sides, and gave his Charge to the Jury in a very impartial Manner. The Jury then withdrew, and was out of Court about two Hours; and on their Return, which was about two o'Clock, on the 8th, in the Morning, gave in their Verdict that fhe was GUILTY, but not of wilful and corrupt Perjury. Upon that Verdict the Court was pleas'd to inform them, that they muft confider what they were about, that they muft either acquit her, or bring her in guilty of the Indictment; they went out a fecond Time, and foon return'd, that fhe was guilty.

Immediately fhe was by the Court committed to *Newgate*, where fhe continu'd till the 30th; then fhe was brought to the Bar again, to receive Sentence in Purfuance of an Adjournment from the 13th. When the Court proceeded to pafs Sentence, which was one Month's Imprifonment, and Tranfportation for feven Years, to one of his Majefty's Colonies in *America*; after hearing every Thing that could be urged in behalf of the Prifoner, to obtain an Arreft of Judgment, or a new

Tryal, by feveral learned Council. There were prefent in Court at that Time the Right Hon. *Thomas Rawlinfon*, Efq; Lord-Mayor of the City of *London*, who always prefides in this Court during the Mayoralty; the Right Hon. Lord Chief Juftice *Willes*, Mr. Juftice *Dennifon*, Mr. Juftice *Clive*, the Barons *Legg* and *Smyth*, and the Recorder, with ten worthy Aldermen, two of which joined in the Judges, *viz.* Mr. Alderman *Janffen*, and Mr. Alderman *Dickinfon*, who all concurred in the above Sentence. The Court was mov'd by Sir *John Barnard*, fenior Alderman, and Member in Parliament for the City of *London*, that the Sentence might be mitigated to fix Months Imprifonment, which met the Approbation of feven more of the Aldermen then prefent, *viz.* Mr. Alderman *Benn*, Sir *Robert Ladbroke*, Mr. Alderman *Alfop*, Mr. Alderman *Cockayne*, Mr. Alderman *Bethell*, Mr. Alderman *Alexander*, and Sir *Richard Glynn*; but was over-rul'd.

In purfuance to her Sentence, fhe was remanded back to *Newgate*. During her Confinement, the great Refort of Perfons occafion'd an Order from the Sheriffs, that Nobody be admitted without their fpecial Licence; after which fhe had the Misfortune to fall dangeroufly ill, as was fuppos'd, by a Gaol Diftemper; whereupon both Phyficians and Surgeons were by fpecial Order fent to vifit her, and by fuch proper Attendance fhe was recovered of her Indifpofition; and on *July* 17th, at the Opening of the Seffions, a Motion was made, that the Court fhould contract with another Perfon, inftead of Mr. *Stewart* (who is the prefent Contracter) for the Tranfportation of Felons, to carry her to *America*; and Mr. *Stewart* in Court confented to wave his Contract; the Motion was granted, on a Divifion, (as we are inform'd) the prefent Contracter being to tranfport her to fome of his Majefty's Colonies in *America*, according to her Sentence, under the ufual Penalty; There were prefent in Favour of this Application, the five following worthy Aldermen, Sir *Robert Ladbroke*, Sir *Jofeph Hankey*, Mr. Alderman *Alfop*, Mr. Alderman *Alexander*, and Mr. Alderman *Scott*; Lord Chief Baron *Parker* and the Recorder againft it. And *July* 20th, about Four in the Afternoon, fhe was by a Warrant directed to the Keeper of *Newgate*, ordering him immediately to deliver her to her Friends, to tranfport herfelf according to the Contract, made and provided in that Cafe; and on *Wednefay, Auguft* the 7th, fhe embark'd on board the *Myrtilda*, Capt. *Budden*, bound for *Philadelphia*.

*Right: Robert Matthew Sully, **Mammy Sally Brown.** Oil on canvas, 31-31/32 × 26-1/16 in. Virginia, c. 1842. Courtesy Massachusetts Historical Society, Boston.*

Sally Brown was clearly a favorite servant of Colonel William Heth of Curles, Virginia. Portraits of servants were extremely rare.

*Opposite: Benjamin Henry Latrobe, **An Overseer doing his duty.** Watercolor, ink, and ink wash on paper, 6-5/16 × 10-5/16 in. Near Fredericksburg, Virginia, 1798. Papers of Benjamin Henry Latrobe, Maryland Historical Society, Baltimore.*

Throughout the period of slavery a primary distinction between white and black women servants was that the latter usually worked in the fields. Some women slaves were trained for domestic service, to work as cooks, nurses, or personal servants, but the majority of southern female slaves lived out their lives as unskilled field hands.

*Below: From the **Massachusetts Gazette & Boston News-Letter,** December 9, 1763. The New-York Historical Society, New York.*

TO BE SOLD,
A likely ſtrong Negro
Girl, about 17 Years of Age; ſold
by Reaſon that a Boy would ſuit
the Owner better. Enquire at
R. & S. Draper's Printing-Office

Women and Religion

Above: Charles Balthazar Julien Fevret de Saint-Memin, **Mrs. Wm. Seaton** (Elizabeth Ann Bayley Seton). Pen and engraving on paper, 2 in. in diam. America, 1797. National Portrait Gallery, Smithsonian Institution, Washington, D.C.

Saint Elizabeth Ann, Roman Catholic convert, was the founder and head of the first American sisterhood, and first American-born Catholic saint.

Opposite: Old Ship Meeting House (built 1681), Hingham, Mass. (Photo: Peggy Barnett)

The people who lived in British North America at the time of the Revolution held a wide variety of religious beliefs, and women had a part in the practices of every denomination.

There was no single religion dominating the native American cultures, just as there was no single religion for the Europeans, yet the ancient matriarchal traditions of the Indians were reflected in their various religious beliefs and practices. In general, the tribal religious leaders, those who received inspired dreams and practiced witchcraft, were men—but not always. Menomini women, for instance, practiced sorcery as freely as the men and were as likely to be sought out by those who wanted protection from evil spirits, predictions of future events, love potions, or medicine to cure disease. Among the Algonquian tribes, on the other hand, female powwows or medicine men were rare. Women always had a role in tribal religious rites, however, and practicing ceremonial dances engaged much of the women's time in many tribes. Female fertility was commonly identified with divinity, and it was thought that seed planted and tended by women was more likely to grow. Among the eastern tribes, tilling ground, growing the crops of corn, beans, squash, and other foodstuffs, was work in which only women participated. In tribes where matriarchal traditions remained strong, as with the Cherokees and Iroquois, the chief of the council of matrons had divine authority and was thought to speak for the Great Spirit when she addressed the warrior chiefs. The tribes of eastern America also recognized a female divinity known as Sky Woman, who, it was said, had created the earth. Sky Woman had had two sons, one good and one evil, and that is why human beings became both good and evil. Native American religion, like that of the Hindus and the ancient Greeks, included many spirits, nature deities, and ghosts, some benevolent and some evil, and religion permeated all facets of life.

Of the religions brought to America by the Europeans, the most ancient was that of the Jews. The first American Jews, two men and one woman, arrived in Virginia in 1624. On the eve of the Revolution approximately fifteen hundred Jews were scattered through the colonies. A visitor to New York City wrote in 1750 that the Jews there lived in "large country seats" and had "several ships, which they load and send out with their own goods." He declared that "they enjoyed all the privileges common to the other inhabitants of this town and province." This was not entirely true, since before the Revolution Jews everywhere were denied the right to vote and hold public office. But since no married women of any religion enjoyed these rights, the status of Jewish women was no different from that of their gentile neighbors in this respect. Marriage outside the faith was not uncommon, but most tried to preserve the ancient beliefs. When her daughter Phila married Oliver De Lancey, who was not Jewish, Bilhah Abigail Franks wrote to her son: "Good God, what a shock it was, when they acquainted me she had left the house and had bin married six months, I can hardly hold my pen whilst I am writting.... Oliver has sent many times to beg leave to see me, but I never would." As for her erring daughter: "I am determined I never will see nor let none of ye family go near her." Nevertheless, another of her children, her son David, soon after also married out of the faith. Among the Jews most ritual takes place in the home where women have a central role, and as the number of Jews in American cities increased, women were found

Above: Anonymous, **Bilhah Abigail Levy Franks.** *Oil on canvas, 44 × 35 in. New York, c. 1740. American Jewish Historical Society, Waltham, Mass. (Photo: Richard Cheek)*

Daughter of a wealthy New York merchant, Bilhah Abigail Levy (1696–1756), founded the first Benevolent Society of the Congregation Shearith Israel in New York.

Opposite: Thomas Sully (attrib.), **Rebecca Gratz** *(1781–1869). Oil on canvas, 20 × 17 in. Philadelphia, begun 1830, Delaware Art Museum, Wilmington.*

Often called the foremost American Jewish woman of her day, the popular but determined spinster founded or helped organize six major charitable societies, among them the first Jewish Sunday school.

at the center of efforts to establish and support synagogues. Bilhah Abigail Franks, known as the "spiritual mother of the women's auxiliaries," organized in New York City a group of Jewish women who donated money, jewelry, and family heirlooms to the fund needed to complete a synagogue.

Jewish women, however, did not restrict their activities to those that would benefit their own group. In Philadelphia in 1801 Rebecca Gratz became involved in charitable activities at the age of twenty when she helped organize the pioneering Female Association for the Relief of Women and Children in Reduced Circumstances. She also helped found the nonsectarian Philadelphia Orphan Asylum. Through Protestant friends she made in these activities, she learned of the Christian Sunday School movement and established a Hebrew Sunday school for Jewish boys and girls. Gratz's religion was no obstacle to her acceptance in Philadelphia society. Indeed, her home was known as a gathering place for distinguished and talented visitors throughout her life.

Catholics faced considerable discrimination in England because theirs was the religion of the traditional French and Spanish enemies. Maryland was established as a refuge for Catholics, but the colony had a Protestant majority and the Catholic population of British North America was concentrated in the settlements originally made by the French in Canada. The most prominent Catholic woman of early America was a convert to the faith. Elizabeth Ann Bayley Seton was born in New York City in 1774, married, and bore five children before her husband died. She was introduced to the teachings of the Catholic Church during a trip to Italy in 1804 and converted the following year. After her conversion she founded a school for wealthy Catholic girls in Baltimore and a few years later, in 1810, another school for poor girls. She was also founder of the Sisters of Charity, the first American Catholic sisterhood, and she has been recognized as the first American-born Catholic saint.

In the wake of the Reformation, a multitude of religious sects had developed in Europe, and a century of religious warfare drove many devout people to America before the Revolution. Germany was the original home of a number of new religious groups dedicated to principles of simplicity, pacifism, and equality for women. Adherents of these groups established their own communities, most of them in Pennsylvania, where they hoped to preserve their own faith undisturbed. These small congregations are described by the general term Pietists, but they all retained their own doctrinal independence. They were distinguished by the leadership roles assumed by the women members of the group and by the formal recognition given to the female part of the congregation.

The Ephrata community, for example, was established in 1732 when two houses were built in what is now Lancaster County, Pennsylvania. One was a "brother house" and the other a "sister house." Although married couples could associate themselves with the church, those living in the brother and sister houses were celibates and in their ascetic mode of life enjoyed perfect equality.

Anonymous, **Marie Elizabeth Blum.** *Oil on wood, 9-3/8 × 6-3/4 in. North Carolina or Pennsylvania, c. 1802–17. Old Salem, Inc. Winston-Salem, N.C. (Photo: Bradford Rauschenberg)*

Moravian women wore tight little caps called **haubes** *fitted with colored strings to indicate their choirs; in this portrait Elizabeth Blum (1743–1817) wears the white ribbons of the widows' choir, her husband, Jacob Blum, a Salem storekeeper, having died in 1802.*

The Moravians are another example. The great woman leader of the group, Anna Nitschmann, spent the years 1740 to 1742 in Pennsylvania attempting to unify the many congregations identified with the German group known as the United Brethren. One of the distinctive practices she introduced was the choir system. The choirs were groups within the congregation which permitted those of various ages and conditions to enjoy self-government. Each choir had its own officers and its own house. There were choirs for widowers, widows, married people, single men, single women, older boys, older girls, little boys, and little girls. Although there was no strict rule governing dress, Moravian women could be recognized by their caps, called *haubes,* tied with different colored ribbons to indicate their choir.

All of the Pietist sects attempted to be directly responsive to the will of God uncontaminated by an intervening structure of ordained priests or formal rituals. The Moravian use of the "lot" to decide important questions illustrates this attitude. To submit a question directly to God, the Moravian elders gathered at a small bowl that contained three reeds. One reed was marked "Ja" for "yes," one was marked "Nein" for "no," and one was a blank. If one of the marked reeds was drawn, the yes or no was accepted as God's answer to the question; if the blank was drawn, it meant that the question had not been asked properly or that it was the sort of question that should not have been put to the lot at all. An important decision for which the lot would be used might involve a proposed marriage between a single "brother" and a single "sister." If the lot went against the match, it would not be made even if both parties and their parents had thought it a good one. No one, however, was required to marry against his or her will.

The Quakers were similar to the German Pietist sects in many ways, sharing a dedication to simplicity, pacifism, and women's rights, but they were of English origin. In an age when the established Protestant churches did not ordain women or permit them to speak, the Society of Friends encouraged women preachers. Among the most prominent of American Quaker preachers was the pious Sophia Hume, who carried her message to the people of Charleston, South Carolina. Her doctrine denouncing luxury and encouraging strict simplicity was also expressed in her books. She wrote *An Exhortation to the Inhabitants of the Province of South-Carolina* in 1748, a plea for repentance and reform, and *A Caution to Such as Observe Days and Times* in 1763, which called for the discontinuance of religious festivals.

Two other sects, heavily influenced by Quaker ideas, were founded in America by women during the eighteenth century. Jemima Wilkinson (1752-1819) began to preach the doctrine of the Universal Friend in 1776, and her preaching

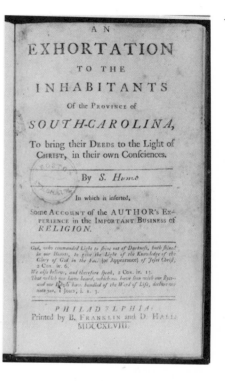

Above:
Sophia Hume, **An Exhortation to the Inhabitants of the Province of South-Carolina, to Bring their Deeds to the Light of Christ, in their own Consciences.** *7-1/2 × 4 in. Printed by B. Franklin and R. Hall, Philadelphia, 1748. Boston Athenaeum.*

Above, left:
Anonymous, **Quaker Meeting.** *Oil on canvas, 25 × 30 in. America, c. 1790. Museum of Fine Arts, Boston. M. and M. Karolik Collection.*

Below, left:
I. Rod Holzhald, **Marriage of 12 Colonial Couples.** *Top section of double engraving, 22 × 15-1/4 in. framed. From a German or French Moravian history, 1757 or 1758. Old Salem, Inc. Winston-Salem, N.C. (Photo: Bradford Rauschenberg)*

In Moravian communities marriages were approved by lot during meetings of the board of church elders.

attracted adherents in Rhode Island, Massachusetts, Connecticut, and Philadelphia. She established a religious settlement called Jerusalem in western New York State. Jemima Wilkinson had no original theological concepts. She preached repentance, the golden rule, and advocated the practice of simplicity, pacifism, and opposition to slavery, all of which were standard Quaker beliefs. But she was an inspiring leader whose followers accepted the one requirement of the sect: "Ye cannot be my friends except ye do whatsoever I command you." Mother Ann Lee—founder of the American branch of the United Society of Believers in Christ's Second Appearing—led a small band of followers to Watervliet, New York (near Albany) in 1776. By the time of her death in 1784 eleven Shaker communities had already been founded. She taught that God is both male and female and recognized equality of the sexes by requiring that each ministry consist of Elders and Elderesses holding equal rank within the internal order of each community. The Shaker emphasis on simplicity and harmony encouraged the development of their distinctive furniture. During religious meetings the early Shakers expressed their ecstasy in violent movements, whirling and shouting. It was from this vigorous form of worship that the sect derived the name by which the "world" called it.

The more conservative Protestant churches to which most American women belonged in the eighteenth century did not allow women much active participation. They might do spinning to help pay the minister, and they were encouraged to practice private devotions and teach religion to their children. But they could not become ministers or preach themselves, and, as the experience of Anne Hutchinson proved, even holding discussion groups for women could be dangerous. Anne Hutchinson had come to Boston from England in 1634. She was a skilled midwife who moved from helping her neighbors with "female problems" to holding group meetings in which the women discussed the ministers' sermons. These groups began to attract husbands and even church elders. Finally Governor Winthrop of Massachusetts reported, "She had more resort to her for counsel about matters of conscience than any minister. I might say than all the elders in the country." She became the center of a theological controversy that split the colony, with leading figures of the community on both sides. In 1638 she was banished from Massachusetts and became one of the founders of the colony of Rhode Island.

Not until the American missionary movement developed at the beginning of the nineteenth century did opportunities for active religious work open up for Protestant women. A group of Congregational women organized the Boston Female Society for Propagating the Diffusion of Christian Knowledge in 1801. A year later, the first of the so-called female "cent" societies was organized, in which members, mainly middle-class women, contributed a penny a week to support missionary activity. As the nineteenth century progressed, women discovered that foreign missions offered opportunities far wider than those available at home. So long as they worked among the heathen, they were permitted to preach and even to practice medicine. Young Harriet Atwood Newell was the first American missionary to die in service. She was only nineteen when she died, but her example served as an inspiration to other women. Eventually the majority of American missionaries were female.

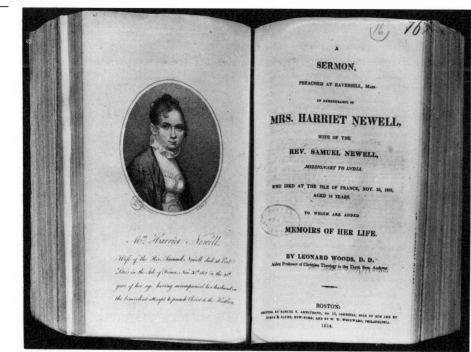

Leonard Woods, D.D., **A Sermon,
Preached at Haverhill in Remembrance of
Mrs. Harriet Newell, Wife of the Rev.
Samuel Newell, Missionary to India ... to
which are added Memoirs of Her Life.**
*6 × 3-1/2 in. 4th ed. Boston, Massachusetts,
1814. Boston Athenaeum.*

*Harriet Atwood Newell, the pioneer
"proto-martyr" of religious missions, was born
in Haverhill and attended several academies
in her youth, experiencing a religious
awakening at the age of 13 or 14. In 1809 she
joined the Haverhill Congregational Church
and two years later married Samuel Newell, a
Harvard graduate dedicated to service as a
missionary in India. She died of consumption
en route to the Isle of France in the Indian
Ocean at the age of 19.*

Harriet Sewall, **The Orphans.** *Watercolor on
paper, 14-3/4 × 21-5/16 in. New England
(?), 1808. Museum of Fine Arts, Boston. M.
and M. Karolik Collection.*

*Toward the end of the 18th century many
Protestant women found an outlet for their
religious impulses by founding or supporting
charities for the relief of widows, orphans, and
the poor.*

Another outlet for the religious impulses of Protestant women was found in charitable organizations. Evidence of women's organizations can be found in America as early as the seventeenth century, but their purposes were economic and political rather than charitable. Toward the end of the eighteenth century, however, the widening social gap between rich and poor made those classes in need of help more conspicuous, and at the same time well-to-do women ceased to be fully employed and were accepting the ladylike code that discouraged women from taking an active interest in politics. The first of the women's charitable organizations was the Society for the Relief of Poor Widows with Small Children, which was founded in New York City in 1797. Similar societies proliferated rapidly. Although the objects of charity were usually widows and orphans, some organizations provided education for free blacks or worked for the manumission of slaves.

The religion of the slaves themselves was a combination of African, native American, and classic Judeo-Christian elements, although it developed as a fundamentally Christian faith. Like the American Indians, the West Africans who were brought to America as slaves believed in a supreme God as well as in a great many specific gods. Despite the trauma of an ocean crossing, they retained beliefs in second sight, ghosts, the influence of spirits, and witchcraft. In the eighteenth century slaves from the West Indies taken to New Orleans introduced voodoo cults, in which women leaders often predominated. The secrecy of voodoo rituals led slave owners to fear that they would lead to slave uprisings, so they suppressed voodoo, which as a consequence never became as strong in North America as it was in the West Indies. But many African beliefs persisted and were integrated with the Christianity the slaves learned from their masters. Belief in spirits and witchcraft was not incompatible with Christianity. Even the Puritans in seventeenth-century Massachusetts had believed sufficiently in spells, levitation, familiar spirits, and the evil eye to execute twenty-eight people as witches.

When given a choice, the slaves preferred the Baptist or Methodist forms of Christianity. They transformed these in their own way and in the eighteenth century encouraged the whites to establish separate congregations for blacks so that they could practice their religion as they chose. Among the slaves, as among the American Indians, doctors as well as preachers were considered religious leaders. Black women who used charms and magic spells, together with drugs and herbal remedies, were respected and sometimes feared. Some of the black medical prescriptions, which included such things as cat soup and boiled cockroaches, were unpleasant and ineffective for anyone who did not have faith in them. Others produced better results than the treatments prescribed by white doctors. In the early eighteenth century slave physicians treated white as well as black patients. Eventually, however, the whites, fearing that the blacks might poison them, outlawed their practice outside the black community. Throughout the period of slavery, however, blacks preferred their own doctors and medico-religious beliefs.

Women at War

Among the Indians of the east coast the influence of women was institutionalized in women's councils. They could veto a declaration of war by refusing to supply moccasins and field rations, and it was recognized that women alone had the right to determine whether a captive taken in war should be killed or adopted into the tribe. In some tribes an individual woman might hold a rank that entitled her to representation in the warriors' council. An example is Nancy Ward (1738-1822) of the Cherokees in Tennessee, who earned her position as "Beloved Woman" by her bravery in battle. In most tribes, women fought only to defend themselves and they did not function as regular warriors, but among the Cherokees it was not unusual for women to take part in battles. A small stream in Georgia was known as "War-woman's Creek" in honor of another Cherokee woman who won a notable victory through a combination of personal bravery and ingenious military strategy.

The political and military influence of white women never equalled that of the Indians. The code of ladylike conduct decreed that both war and politics were outside the sphere of women. In early America, however, women were intimately involved in both.

By the time of the Revolution, the ladylike ideal had begun to make some inroads in America, but both working women and would-be ladies displayed little hesitation in making their political opinions known. The printer Mary Katharine Goddard accepted a commission from the Continental Congress to print the first edition of the Declaration of Independence bearing the names of those men willing to pledge their "lives, fortunes, and sacred honor" to the cause of American freedom. Contrary to popular belief, the Declaration of Independence was adopted but not signed in July 1776, and it was not until Goddard printed her edition in January 1777 that all of the men who had signed during the intervening months were publicly identified. Other women freely expressed their views on such politically charged subjects as tea drinking. In 1774 the *Virginia Gazette* published "A Lady's Adieu to her Tea Table":

> Farewell the Tea Board, with its gaudy Equipage,
> Of Cups and Saucers, Cream Bucket, Sugar Tongs,
> The pretty Tea Chest also, lately stor'd
> With Hysen, Congo, and best Double Fine.
> Full many a joyous Moment have I sat by ye,
> Hearing the Girls' Tattle, the Old Maids talk Scandal,
> And the spruce Coxcomb laugh at—maybe—Nothing.
> No more shall I dish out the once lov'd Liquor,
> Though now detestable,
> Because I'm taught (and I believe it true)
> Its use will fasten slavish Chains upon my Country,
> And LIBERTY's the Goddess I would choose
> To reign triumphant in AMERICA.

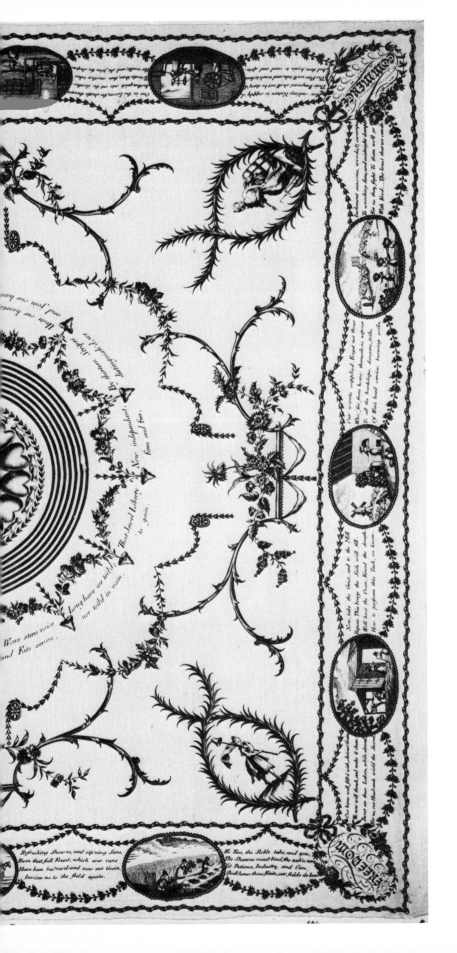

Printed Handkerchief. Red copper-plate printing on cotton, 26 in. square. England, 1784–1800. Concord Antiquarian Society, Mass.

This unusual English handkerchief was undoubtedly printed for the American market, for it commemorates the daily pursuits of three industrious sisters who turned to husbandry while their husbands fought for American independence. The central design, an anchor surrounded by hearts and clasped hands, features a poem celebrating liberty and independence. The border design contains thirteen medallions – each with appropriate verse – that portray the three sisters engaged in various agricultural and commercial activities: spinning and weaving cloth for the soldiers, taking food to camp, plowing the fields, harvesting crops, curing tobacco for export, milling, and baking. The story ends happily in the final medallion which finds the husbands safe and reunited with their families in 1783.

As with the men, a good many women were not sympathetic to the patriot cause. Hannah Griffitts of Philadelphia, after reading Tom Paine's popular pamphlet, "The Crisis," penned these lines:

> Pane—Tho' thy tongue may now run glibber
>   Warm'd with thy Independent glow
> Thou art indeed the Coldest fibber
>   I ever knew—or wish to know.

Mercy Otis Warren, who was often troubled by her own lapses from the ladylike ideal, nevertheless assured John Adams that American ladies would not grow so indifferent to politics as to endanger the principles of the Revolution. "Your asking my opinion on so momentous a point as the form of government which ought to be preferred by a people about to shake off the fetters of monarchic and aristocratic tyranny," she wrote in 1776, "may be designed to ridicule the sex for paying any attention to political matters. Yet I shall venture to give you a serious reply. Notwithstanding the love of dress, dancing, and equipage, notwithstanding the fondness for finery, folly and fashion, is so strongly predominant in the female mind, I hope never to see a Monarchy established in America."

Certainly many American ladies willingly joined the war effort after fighting had begun. As in earlier wars, women's organizations, now often calling themselves "daughters of liberty," sewed, knitted, and spun for the American troops. "The Association," the largest women's wartime organization, was founded in Philadelphia by Esther DeBerdt Reed (1746-1780). After Reed's death, Sarah Franklin Bache (1743-1802) and four other women formed a committee to take over direction of the group. There is evidence of Association activity in six states. Meanwhile many women suffered for their political views during the war. Loyalist women might lose their homes and property, and patriot women frequently became the victims of politically motivated rape. During the 1776 campaign in New Jersey, the British policy of destruction and devastation included attacks on women. A letter published in the *Pennsylvania Evening Post* reported several events which were typical:

> Since I wrote to you this morning I have had an opportunity of hearing a number of the particulars of the horrid depredations committed by that part of the British army which was stationed at and near Penny-town, under the command of Lord Cornwallis. Besides the sixteen women who had fled to the woods to avoid their brutality and were there seized and carried off, one man had the cruel mortification to have his wife and only daughter (a child of ten years of age) ravished... another girl of thirteen years of age was taken from her father's house, carried to a barn about a mile, there ravished, and afterwards made use of by five more of these brutes. Numbers of instances of the same kind of behavior I am assured of have happened....

In Congress, July 4, 1776, the unanimous Declaration of the Thirteen United States of America. *Broadside, 26 × 21 in. matted. Mary Katharine Goddard, Baltimore, 1777. The Library of Congress, Washington, D.C.*

In January 1777 Congress ordered an authentic copy of the Declaration to be printed and distributed to each of the thirteen states. The commission went to the Baltimore printer and patriot Mary Katharine Goddard. The proof printing shown here (see detail) bears John Hancock's authorizing signature as "A True Copy."

IN CONGRESS, JANUARY 18, 1777.

ECLARATION OF INDEPENDENCY, with the Names of the MEMBERS of CONGR
they be desired to have the same put on RECORD.

By Order of CO

A True Copy

JOHN HAN

John Hancock Presid

BALTIMORE, in MARYLAND: Printed by MARY KATHARINE GODDARD.

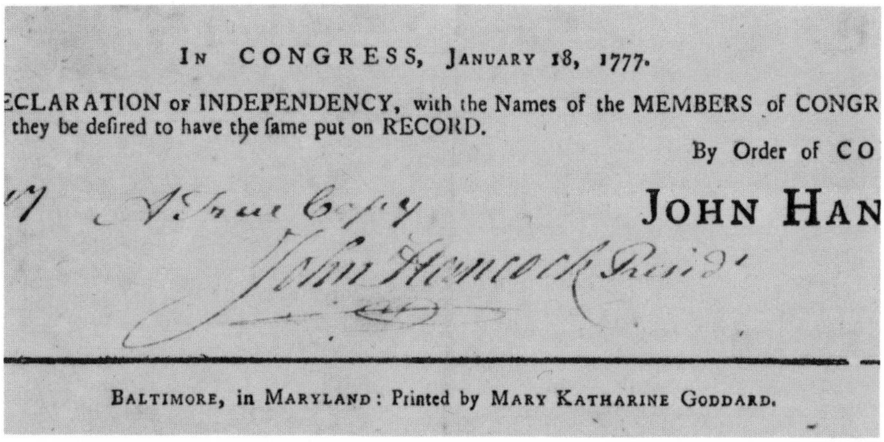

Right: ***An Address to New-England: Written by a Daughter of Liberty.*** *Broadside, 14-3/4 × 8-7/8 in. Boston, 1774. Historical Society of Pennsylvania, Philadelphia. (Photo: Joseph Kelley)*

This patriotic broadside mourns the fate of "Unhappy Boston" at the hands of the British. The anonymous author urged her compatriots to consider "What Sins, what crying Sins" had provoked God to punish this "Backsliding Land." She advised New England to "turn unto thy God, Fear not the Tyrant's Yoke nor threatning Rod."

An ADDRESS to NEW-ENGLAND:

WRITTEN BY

A DAUGHTER of LIBERTY.

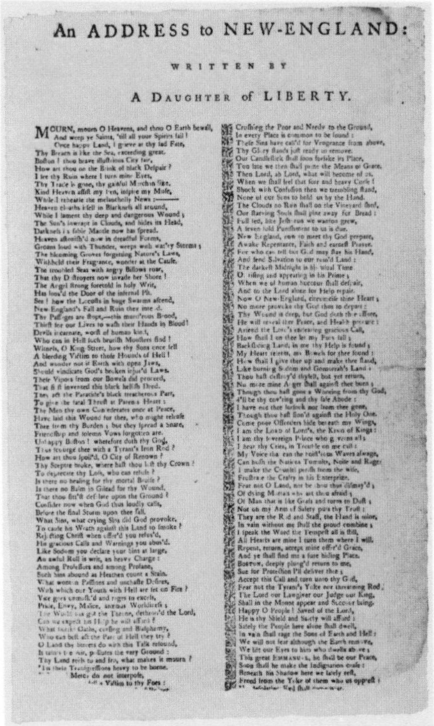

Far right: Elisha Fish, ***Joy and Gladness: a Thanksgiving Discourse... occasioned by the Repeal of the Stamp Act.*** *7-7/8 × 5 in. Printed by Sarah Goddard and Company, Providence, Rhode Island, 1767. Library of the Rhode Island Historical Society, Providence.*

JOY and GLADNESS:

A

Thanksgiving DISCOURSE,

Preached in UPTON,

WEDNESDAY, MAY 28, 1766;

OCCASIONED BY THE

REPEAL

OF THE

STAMP-ACT.

BY

ELISHA FISH, A.M.

Pastor of the CHURCH there.

PROVIDENCE, in NEW-ENGLAND:

Printed and sold by Sarah Goddard, and Company, at the Post-Office.

M,DCC,LXVII.

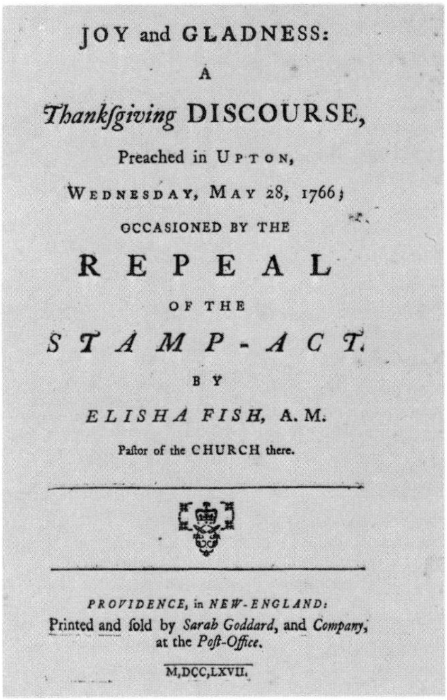

After the death of her physician husband in Groton, Connecticut, Sarah Updike Goddard (c. 1700–70) moved to join her son, William, in Providence in 1762 when he started the ***Providence Gazette.*** *In 1765 he turned the press over to his mother, and she ran it until 1768 when she sold the business and rejoined her son in Philadelphia.*

*Anonymous, **The Takeing of Miss Mud Islnd**. Engraving, 8-15/16 × 7-1/4 in. London, c. December 1777. Trustees of the British Museum, London.*

Warfare during the colonial period rarely involved engagements between conventional armies. Most of the action, even during the Revolution, took place in small skirmishes involving irregular militia units and Indians. In these actions women used hatchets, muskets, farm implements, and even such improvised weapons as pots of boiling lye to defend their homes and families. Such women were viewed as a sort of auxiliary to the male militia units and many of the best-known heroines of the war are remembered for such activities. For instance, sixteen-year-old Sybil Ludington rode horseback forty miles on the night of April 26, 1777, to rouse the local militia to the defense of Danbury, Connecticut. Nancy Hart of Georgia is known for her capture of five British soldiers whom she held at gunpoint until the arrival of American troops. Grace and Rachel Martin captured a British courier and two officers and sent the documents they carried to General Nathaniel Greene. Behethland Moore, a fifteen-year-old from South Carolina, made another "midnight" ride to carry a message to an American captain.

In addition, however, the American Revolution involved many women in the activities of the regular Continental armies. The great length of the war and the widely extended movements of the British army created thousands of women refugees who sought safety with the American troops. Most often these were wives or widows of enlisted men whose farms or other means of livelihood had been destroyed by the British. The most prominent camp followers were the wives of high-ranking officers who could afford to provide reasonably comfortable quarters for them and their children at camp. These included Martha Washington and the wives of General Greene and General Knox. But lower-ranking officers and all but the poorest enlisted men left their wives at home to keep the farms and shops. Only desperately poor women voluntarily shared the hardships of camp life with the enlisted men.

Washington could not turn these homeless women and their children away, and even when they exceeded the number of camp followers needed for the proper functioning of the army, he allowed them half rations for themselves and quarter rations for each child. Although these women were poor, they did not become prostitutes. The British army accepted the presence of "camp wives" for officers, and they had the money to pay for such services. But the American officers would not tolerate adultery among their ranks, and the enlisted men did not have enough money even to keep themselves clothed and fed. Although the hardships of war did drive some women into prostitution, they practiced this profession in the cities occupied by the British, not in American army camps.

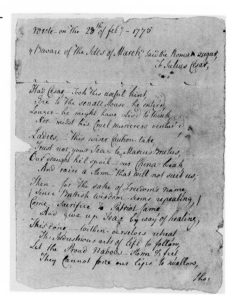

Yet there was a good deal of "women's work" to be done in the American army, especially nursing. In 1778 Dr. James Craik, chief physician and surgeon of the Continental Army, wrote, "I wish some method could be fallen upon to employ women that can be depended on. The General says we may enlist them for at least the same money as are paid soldiers, for he can no longer bear having an army on paper and not have them in the field."

In addition to the usual camp women's occupations—cooking, mending uniforms and stockings, foraging, nursing, and doing laundry—the women had special assignments during battle. The most important of these was carrying water to the cannon so that they could be swabbed out after each firing. When a gun crew was short a man, the woman who usually brought the water knew enough about the work to fill in. As the activities of these Revolutionary women faded into myth, they came to be known by the generic name "Molly Pitcher." This name never appears in a source before 1859, and it is fruitless to hunt for the "real" Molly Pitcher. Mary Hays of Carlisle, Pennsylvania, was one of many women present during the battle of Monmouth, but there is no reason to identify her with either of the two women who were seen handling weapons on that occasion. In many ways, however, she was typical of the women who followed the American armies. She was a poor woman who had gone to work as a domestic servant when she was about fifteen and in the same year had married a barber. He enlisted in the American army in 1775, and when her employer became commander of the same unit in 1778, Hays joined her husband at camp. After the war, they settled in Pennsylvania. When she was widowed, Hays married another Revolutionary war veteran named John McCauley. When he too died, she supported herself for the rest of her life working as a charwoman, with her small earnings supplemented by a Pennsylvania pension granted "for her services during the revolutionary war." Those services very probably included carrying water to the cannon as well as nursing and doing laundry. Margaret Corbin, a camp follower whose wartime activities definitely included at least one day of service at a field piece, was also a very poor woman. She was wounded during action at Fort Washington in 1776, and her husband was killed in the same engagement. Widowed and crippled for life, Margaret Corbin became the first woman to collect a federal pension as compensation for her disability, and she is the only Revolutionary veteran to be buried at West Point.

At least a few women who preferred soldiering to nursing disguised themselves as men and drew full pay and rations as regular troops. The best known of these is Deborah Sampson (later Gannett) of Massachusetts, who revealed the details of her service in public lectures after the war. Since she remained a poor woman all her life, she anxiously sought all possible income from lectures, books, and pensions. Other women who got away with similar masquerades were more reticent, and their army experiences are documented only in the most fragmentary records or not at all. Deborah Gannett succeeded in obtaining a federal pension during her lifetime, and after her death Congress adopted an "Act for the relief of the heirs of Deborah Gannett, a soldier of the Revolution, deceased." She enlisted under the name of Robert Shurtleff. She was a strong woman of above average height; her military performance fully satisfied her officers. During an engagement near Tarrytown, New York, she was wounded

Anonymous, *A Society of Patriotic Ladies,
at Edenton in North Carolina. Mezzotint,
13-1/8 × 10 in. London, March 25, 1775.
Trustees of the Boston Public Library. (Photo
courtesy Metropolitan Museum of Art, New
York)*

*This English political cartoon satirizes the
occasion when, on October 25, 1774, 51 of the
leading women of the Albemarle region in
North Carolina gathered in Edenton and
drew up a resolution boycotting "East India
tea" and all taxed British goods.*

*Opposite:
Fidelia [Hannah Griffitts],* **Beware of the
Ides of March....***Autograph manuscript
poem, 8-1/2 × 6-1/2 in. Philadelphia,
February 28, 1775. Library Company of
Philadelphia. (Photo: Joseph Kelley)*

*Little is known about the life of the
Philadelphia Quaker woman who wrote this
sophisticated verse urging support of the
colonial boycott of British imports. Hannah
Griffitts (1727–1817) was associated with
leading upper-class families of Philadelphia,
and none of her work has yet been identified in
published form. However, due to the intensely
political nature of her subject matter –
unusual for a woman poet of that era – it is
possible that poems were published
anonymously or under the pseudonym she
sometimes favored, "Fidelia."*

Above: Joseph Stone, **Deborah Sampson**
*[Gannett]. Oil on paper, 17-1/2 × 13-1/2 in.
framed. Framingham, Massachusetts, 1797.
Rhode Island Historical Society, Providence.*

Left: John Hoppner, R.A., **Sarah Franklin Bache.** *Oil on canvas, 30-1/8 × 24-7/8 in. London, 1797. Metropolitan Museum of Art, New York. Wolfe Fund, 1901.*

Sarah Franklin Bache (1743–1808), daughter of Benjamin and Deborah (Read) Franklin, was a leader of the "Association," an interstate patriotic women's organization that supplied money and clothing for the war effort.

Right: Spinning wheel. Colonial Williamsburg Foundation, Williamsburg, Va. (Photo: Peggy Barnett)

During the Revolution the patriots' boycott of British textiles – England's major industry – was considered a crippling weapon to use against the mother country. From the early colonial days American women had gathered to spin and weave in groups, and with the escalation of hostilities in the 1760s and 1770s, patriotic "daughters of Liberty" employed their spinning wheels in a concerted effort to support domestic industry.

The Sentiments of an American Woman. *Broadside, 13-5/8 × 8-1/2 in. Philadelphia, June 10, 1780. Historical Society of Pennsylvania, Philadelphia. (Photo: Joseph Kelley)*

This eloquent patriotic broadside speaks of the gratitude of American women toward "the valiant defenders of America" in the Army. It was widely distributed by members of the "Association," an organization of women formed by Esther Reed, wife of Pennsylvania Governor Joseph Reed. The purpose of the "Association" was to solicit donations of money from women to be presented to the soldiers as "the offering of the Ladies."

A New Touch on the Times. Well adapted to the distressing Situation of every Sea-port Town. By a Daughter of Liberty, living in Marblehead. Broadside, 13 × 8-1/4 in. Massachusetts, 1779. The New-York Historical Society.

This wartime broadside describes in heartfelt, if halting, verse the deprivations of the civilian population during the Revolution. The woodcut of the female Continental soldier decorating the upper right-hand corner was used again, less appropriately, on a broadside printed in 1793 concerned with "the horrid and barbarous Execution of the late unfortunate Monarch, Louis XVIth of France."

Opposite:
James Calhoun, Jr. (Deputy Commissary of Fort McHenry), **Receipt to Mary Pickersgill for Making Flags.** *Autograph manuscript, 5 × 7 in. Baltimore, August 19, 1813. The Star Spangled Banner Flag House Association, Inc., Baltimore, Md.*

In 1813 Major George Armistead, Commandant of Fort McHenry, commissioned Mary Pickersgill, a flagmaker and an "exceedingly patriotic woman," to make a "flag so large that the British will have no difficulty in seeing it from a distance." The Baltimore widow, working with the assistance of her mother, Rebecca Young, and other family members, reputedly used more than 400 yards of bunting to construct the banner, which measured 30 × 42 feet and cost $405.90 to complete.

but treated the injury herself in order to prevent the discovery that she was a woman. Her sex was finally discovered when she was hospitalized with a fever, and she was discharged from the service in October 1783.

After the Revolution the United States enjoyed almost thirty years of peace. When an invading British army again appeared in America during the War of 1812, women's participation was far more restricted than it had been during the Revolution. An interesting volume was produced after the war by a writer using the name Louisa Baker, claiming to be the memoirs of a woman born in Plymouth County, Massachusetts, who served for three years as a sailor on the frigate *Constitution*. Although the story is not implausible, it is suspect because no corroborating evidence for any part of it has been found. In this war, in fact, sewing the flag that flew at Fort McHenry in Baltimore was probably the outstanding feminine achievement.

It is curious that Betsy Ross should be the best-known woman of the Revolutionary War era, an age filled with flamboyantly active heroines. Ross was a Philadelphia upholsterer who, like all working women, took any kind of work that was offered her. In 1777 she made a few flags for the Philadelphia navy; these may have been signal flags, Pennsylvania state flags, or possibly some form of Stars and Stripes. In 1870, more than three decades after her death, her grandson first told the story that has given her fame. According to his version of what had become family legend, Betsy Ross had been visited in her upholstery shop in June 1776 by George Washington and other members of a secret committee who asked her to design and make a flag for the nation that was soon to declare its independence. There is, however, no evidence whatever to corroborate this story. When Washington took command of the American army at Cambridge, Massachusetts, in July 1775, he raised a flag that had the British crosses of St. George and St. Andrew in the corner and six horizontal white stripes on a red field. He was still with the army, in New York, a year later when his alleged conversation with Betsy Ross would have taken place. In June 1777 Congress passed its Flag Act, which decreed that the American naval flag include thirteen red and white stripes and thirteen white stars in a blue field. Flagmakers had considerable discretion as to how they would interpret this. Scholars now believe that the so-called Bennington Flag, which is only nine stripes wide and has an arch of eleven seven-pointed stars over the numerals "76" with two more stars in the top corners of the field, is the first Stars and Stripes flag to have been used by an American army. It is believed to have been used at the Battle of Bennington in August 1777. No one knows who made it, but since soldiers knew how to do simple sewing, it is not inconceivable that it was run up by one of the men. The making of flags was not considered a particularly important activity during the Revolution; in 1813 it was. The most famous early American flagmaker should be Mary Young Pickersgill, whose extraordinarily impressive feat of needlework produced a flag forty-two feet long and thirty feet high with each of its fifteen stars measuring two feet from point to point. It was this Fort McHenry flag that came to be known as "Old Glory" and inspired Francis Scott Key to compose our national anthem, "The Star Spangled Banner."

Accomplished Women

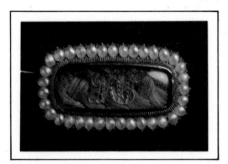

Above: **Handkerchief Pin.** *Gold, pearls, hair, glass, 3/8· × 1-1/8 × 1-1/4 in. Massachusetts, 1812. Courtesy Massachusetts Historical Society, Boston. (Photo: Peggy Barnett)*

Mercy Otis Warren's **History of the ... Revolution** *(1805) caused a serious breach between the noted writer and her long-time friend John Adams, who was offended by her portrayal of him. Adams was moved to complain that "History is not the Province of Ladies." The two exchanged a series of heated letters and were not reconciled until 1812. The Adamses made up with Mercy Warren through a mutual exchange of hair, which Abigail Adams had made into jewelry to symbolize their renewed friendship. This pin was the one worn by Abigail Adams.*

Opposite: John Singleton Copley, **Mercy Otis Warren.** *Oil on canvas, 51-1/4 × 41 in. Boston, c. 1763. Museum of Fine Arts, Boston. Bequest of Winslow Warren.*

Mercy Otis Warren (1728–1814) whose home in Plymouth became a salon for Americans voicing political dissent during the Revolution, was a poet, playwright, historian, and political satirist.

One of the luxuries desired by Americans who had accumulated some wealth and had begun to emulate the style of life of upper-class Europeans was an education beyond the practical that would mark them as persons of taste and culture. Practical education included the skills needed to earn a living, which, for women, meant all the housewifely arts as well as some special abilities required in the family business. Religious and political ideals dictated that all children should learn to read the Bible and enough history and current news to make them virtuous citizens. Youngsters also were taught sufficient arithmetic to enable them to keep accounts and make the measurements necessary in their work.

Only a few occupations in early America required education beyond these basics. Clergymen, lawyers, and physicians who wished to study the works of the ancients had to read both Latin and Greek, but knowledge of a classical language was a luxury for others. Writing, too, for most people, was an inessential skill and a relatively expensive one to learn. Paper and ink were costly, and mastering the manipulation of a goose-quill pen and techniques necessary to keep it in repair with a penknife were time-consuming. Consequently many Americans of the eighteenth century who could read did not know how to write. Elegant penmanship and the ability to spell and punctuate correctly were the first American "accomplishments."

Upper-class children whose parents wished them to become ladies and gentlemen usually began their educations at home just as those of poorer families did. And as in poorer families, the mother was the first teacher. As wealthy children grew up, a tutor to supplement the mother's instruction was often hired. Upper-class daughters, in that case, might receive training in the classics, history, and science along with their brothers. Dr. Benjamin Rush gave a lecture in 1787 entitled "Thoughts upon Female Education, Accommodated to the Present State of Society, Manners, and Government in the United States of America," in which he suggested that teaching girls serious subjects was utilitarian, since they would later pass on their knowledge to their sons. He warned against females wasting too much time on accomplishments like music that were important to European ladies but inappropriate luxuries in America.

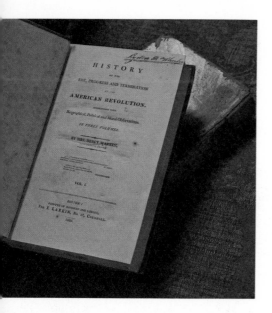

Mercy Otis Warren, **History of the Rise, Progress, and Termination of the American Revolution.** *...Vol. I. Boston, Manning and Loring, 1805. The Pilgrim Society, Plymouth, Mass. (Photo: Peggy Barnett)*

This major work was begun in the 1770s and took nearly thirty years to complete. The three-volume history angered New England Federalists with its Jeffersonian views favoring popular government; however, the author, who had been active in Massachusetts political circles throughout the Revolution, provided valuable firsthand accounts of major events and personal assessments of the people involved in fostering the cause of independence.

Consequently, upper-class girls in America in the eighteenth century received educations much more similar to those given boys than was the case in Europe, although females were barred from attending the few colleges that then existed for male students. A few exceptional American women nevertheless managed to develop into genuinely learned ladies. Jane Colden became a respected botanist under the tutelage of her father, who was a doctor of medicine. Although she never learned Latin, she learned to describe plants in English and in 1757 completed a catalogue of New York flora. Her father was so proud of her work that he introduced her to his friends in the international scientific community. She won fame as "perhaps the only lady that makes profession of the Linnaean system." Hannah Adams of Massachusetts learned Latin and Greek from some of the boarders in her family's home. She did not marry and, faced with the need to make a living, she tried tutoring boys preparing for college and also making lace. Finally she hit upon the idea of publishing a scholarly manuscript which she had been working on for her own pleasure. *An Alphabetical Compendium of the Various Sects* was published in 1784 and was praised for the wide range of sources the author had used as well as for her impartiality. From then on, Adams sought to make a living through her scholarship and was partially successful, although her earnings from her *History of the Jews* and other books had to be supplemented by an annuity provided for her by her friends. Mercy Otis Warren of Plymouth, Massachusetts, received her education by sitting in on the lessons provided by her brothers' tutor as they were prepared for college. She was an active propagandist for the patriot cause and became best known for her satirical plays. The first of these, *The Adulator,* appeared in 1772. Warren also wrote poetry, and, in 1788, a political tract entitled "Observations on the New Constitution." Her most important work is a three-volume *History of the Rise, Progress and Termination of the American Revolution,* which she began during the war and published in 1805. The education of Theodosia Burr was supervised by her father, Aaron Burr, near the end of the century when more and more upper-class girls were being educated in the European style. She was also taught serious subjects rather than ornamental ones, in order, her father said, "to convince the world what neither sex appear to believe—that women have souls!"

To be cultivated as European ladies were, however, a girl did not study the same subjects as men. Those seeking gentility would not have been flattered by this description of some New England women written in 1781:

> The women of Connecticut are...to be compared to the prude rather than the European polite lady. They are not permitted to read plays; cannot converse about whist, quadrille, or operas; but will freely talk upon the subjects of history, French, geography, and mathematics. They are great causists and polemical divines; and I have known not a few of them so well schooled in Greek and Latin as often to put to the blush learned gentlemen.

John Vanderlyn (attrib.), **Theodosia Burr.** *Oil on canvas, 22 × 26-3/16 in. New York, 1815–20. The New-York Historical Society.*

Beloved daughter of the brilliant but controversial politician Aaron Burr and his wife, Theodosia Bartow Prevost, Theodosia Burr (Mrs. Joseph Alston, 1783–1813) is remembered as one of the most accomplished and learned women of her day. This unfinished portrait is one of several of her painted by Vanderlyn during the early 19th century.

Left: Chester Harding, **Hannah Adams.** *Oil on canvas, 36 × 27 in. Boston (?), 827. c. 1827. Boston Althenaeum.*

Hannah Adams (1755–1831) was the first American woman who tried to support herself by her writings, which included religious chronologies such as **The History of the Jews.**

Right: Anonymous, **A Ceremonial at a Young Ladies Seminary.** *Oil on canvas, 30 × 39 in. American, 1800–10. Colonel Edgar William and Bernice Chrysler Garbisch.*

Below, right: **The New-England Primer Improved....***Providence, Rhode Island, John Waterman, 1775. Robert Hudson, Tannahile Research Library, Greenfield Village and Henry Ford Museum, Dearborn, Mich.*

Below, left: Linden Hall Seminary for Young Ladies, **Terms and Conditions of the Boarding School for Female Education in Litiz…January 6, 1809.** *Lancaster, Pennsylvania, 1808 (?). Historical Society of Pennsylvania, Philadelphia. (Photo: Joseph Kelley)*

Consequently, women as well as men enthusiastically welcomed the proliferation of schools for young ladies in the last quarter of the eighteenth century, which offered special instruction in feminine accomplishments. Many finishing schools, academies, and female seminaries had facilities to accommodate boarders as well as day students. Among the best were the Moravian schools at Bethlehem, Pennsylvania, and at Salem, North Carolina. Daughters who were unable to attend such institutions might acquire some of the same polish by taking private lessons in music, dance, painting, needlework, or a language from one of the many individuals who offered such instruction. As late as 1786, an advertisement in the *Virginia Independent Chronicle* described a new boarding school that emphasized the advantages of co-education. Except for special Saturday classes in which the girls would "be taught plain Needle Work, and the Duties incumbent on the Mistresses of Families," the schoolmaster announced that "No other Difference will be made between the Education of Boys and Girls, except that the Girls will not be taught Mathematics." He believed both sexes would perform better under a system that would "excite a greater emulation in both." The code of ladylike behavior, however, deplored such competition. A lady who wished to attract a gentlemanly husband must acknowledge his superiority in all things, and if her talents should be superior to his, she must do everything in her power to conceal the fact. Co-education was a poor training ground for such behavior, and by the end of the century such arrangements were virtually unheard of. In 1794 an advertisement for a young ladies' academy in Maryland stated, "The superior advantages, which institutions of this kind have over those schools…whose regulations admit both sexes, are too apparent to need a comment." Affluent Americans soon came to agree that girls had "equal" educational opportunities only if they had the same chance to become ladies in the European style as their brothers had to become gentlemen.

Schools for would-be ladies taught the basics of reading, arithmetic, spelling, fine penmanship, geography, French, and sometimes the classics. Instead of reading history and politics, however, ladies read moral tracts, plays, poetry, and novels. These last often seemed a bit naughty to American women, but if they ended with virtue rewarded and vice punished they were tolerated. Indeed, the habit of reading novels could become addictive. Elizabeth Drinker of Pennsylvania noted in her diary in January 1796, "It may appear strange to some that an infirm old woman should begin the year reading romances—'tis a practice I by no means highly approve; yet I trust I have not sinned, as I read a little of most things." Girls also learned the ornamental skills of music—they learned to sing as well as to play such instruments as the guitar, violin, harpsichord, and the newly invented piano—dancing, painting, drawing, and fine needlework.

Needlework was a matter of high priority at these schools, where a mastery of various embroidery stitches was considered a necessary achievement for proper young ladies of station. By the mid-1700s advertisements for instruction in needlework were common in newspapers. On August 21, 1755, Elizabeth Hinche advertised in the *Boston Weekly News-Letter* that she "doth teach plain Sewing, Irish Stitch, Ten Stitch, Sampler Work, Embroidery, and other Sorts of Needle Work: If any Person sees fit to send their Children from the Country to School and Board, she will provide for them in a decent Manner...." Although girls since the earliest days of colonization had been taught plain sewing at home or at local schools, fine needle arts required years of training, and it was in the female academies that flourished at the end of the eighteenth century that these techniques were taught. In fact, the best visual record we have of these schools is in the finely worked samplers and needlework pictures that were executed as part of each young lady's training. Students were expected to work a series of samplers or "exemplers," each one a record of different embroidery stitches, as well as an effective exercise in the letters of the alphabet, sayings from the Bible, and moral truisms. Girls usually began with a simple alphabet sampler worked in elementary cross-stitch and then advanced into more difficult exercises, using a greater variety of stitches, such as running, satin, stem, chain, tent, and bullion. Samplers of the seventeenth and early eighteenth centuries were generally long and narrow with the primary design focusing on parallel rows of numbers and letters, but by the late 1700s the shape had become almost square, with designs incorporating embroidered figures, plants, and animals, as well as buildings and pastoral landscapes. Samplers and needlework pictures worked at various schools usually shared design elements, thanks to the influence of the individual teachers.

Anonymous, **Terrestrial Globe.** *Silk and ink on silk, 6-1/2 in. in diam. Chester County, Pennsylvania, 1810–20. Chester County Historical Society, West Chester, Pa. (Photo: Peggy Barnett)*

The Westtown School, opened in 1799 and operated by the Society of Friends, instructed entering students to bring with them "a pair of Scissors, Thread-case, Thimble, Work-bag and some plain sewing or knitting to begin with." In keeping with instructions at similar schools, the girls worked alphabets and needlework pictures, but they also made darning-and-mending samplers and celestial and terrestrial globes.

Opposite: Ann Marsh, **Sampler.** *Silk on linen, 17 × 13-1/4 in. Philadelphia (?), 1727. George Norman Highley. (Photo: Peggy Barnett)*

An interesting assortment of embroidery survives from the hand of Ann Marsh (1717–97), an exceptional needlewoman who is known to have taught needlework in Philadelphia before she retired to Willistown, Pennsylvania. She was born in England but came to Philadelphia in 1727 and may have worked this sampler there when she was only ten.

poor state of iacob here it seems to me his cattle for was soft
yet god a peared there his ioy his crown god is not all ways for
where the contented mind is known. there is a sweet increase
of solace where the soul lies down in everlasting peace
vertue seeks not for praise of man true glory is its due
which fleeting envy never can dispel from vertue true

Left: Nabby (Abigail) Martin, **Sampler.**
*Silk on canvas, 15 × 10-1/4 in. Providence,
Rhode Island, 1786. Museum of Art, Rhode
Island School of Design, Providence. (Photo
courtesy of E. P. Dutton, Inc.)*

Among the most beautiful embroideries done at
American schools during the 18th century are
the samplers stitched at Miss Mary Balch's
school in Providence (founded before 1785
and lasting until 1831). They are acclaimed
for their architectural views and the quality of
needlework; here Nabby pictured both
University Hall at Brown University (begun
1764) and the Providence State House
(1762–1900). She was the daughter of
Sylvanus Martin, a Revolutionary War
soldier and member of the Assembly.

Opposite, left: Lydia Church (age 13), **Sampler**
*(detail). Silk, sequins, and metallic threads on
linen, 18-3/4 × 20-3/4 in. Worked at Mrs.
Mansfield's school, New Haven, Connecticut,
1791. The Connecticut Historical Society,
Hartford.*

Like many other late 18th-century schoolgirl
samplers, this example incorporates a building
and figures surrounded by an elaborate floral
border.

Opposite, right: Anonymous, **Sampler.**
*Silk and linen on linen, 14 × 9 in. Chester
County, Pennsylvania, 1790. Chester County
Historical Society, West Chester, Pa. (Photo:
Peggy Barnett)*

A group of samplers worked in the Chester
County and Philadelphia area during the
second half of the 18th century incorporate
lace inserts such as hollie point and drawn
work. Certainly one of the most elaborate
examples of this type is the sampler shown here,
worked by an unidentified "IG." Although
several all-white versions are known, the
surface of this sampler is covered with brilliant
polychrome silk embroidery.

Above: Elizabeth Alston Williams (attrib.), **Landscape.** *Watercolor on silk, 21-5/8 × 20-7/8 in. Winston-Salem, North Carolina, c. 1815. Private collection. (Photo: Bradford Rauschenberg)*

Although schools in the rural South offered instruction for young ladies, few examples of southern needlework survive. The Salem Female Academy was founded by the Moravians in Salem, North Carolina, on April 23, 1772, and expanded to take in boarders in 1802, charging an annual rate of $160 to $180. As in northern schools, girls between eight and twelve were taught reading, grammar, writing, arithmetic, history, geography, and plain needlework. Music, drawing, and fine needlework were available at extra cost. Elizabeth Williams of Warren, North Carolina, was enrolled from May 8, 1812, until 1816. The painted floral border is typical of contemporary Moravian needlework.

Right: Ann Marsh, **Needlework Picture.** *Silk on satin with silk border, 17-1/2 × 10-1/4 in. Pennsylvania (?), 1727–60. Mrs. Lynmar Brock. (Photo: Peggy Barnett)*

Geography exercise, Salem Female Academy. Old Salem, Inc. Winston-Salem, N.C. (Photo: Peggy Barnett)

*Opposite, far left: Persis Crane, **Wisdom-Leading Youth to Education** (detail). Silk on silk, 18-1/2 × 15 in. Dorchester, Massachusetts, 1812. Mr. and Mrs. Bertram K. Little. (Photo: Richard Cheek)*

Although young ladies embroidered needlework pictures during the 18th century, the form really flourished during the early years of the Republic. Some of the most elegant examples, such as this one, were executed at Mrs. Saunders' and Miss Beach's school in Dorchester after it opened in 1803.

*Opposite, above: Prudence Perkins, **River Townscape with Figures**. Watercolor and ink on paper, 18-1/2 × 22-3/4 in. Providence (?), 1810. Peter H. Tillou. (Photo courtesy Whitney Museum of American Art, New York)*

Most pictures painted by schoolgirls at the female academies early in the 19th century show a decided kinship with embroideries. The trees here, for example, are closer to their silk chenille-work counterparts in contemporary needlework pictures than they are to nature. Like many schoolgirl drawings, this landscape owes its success to a strong sense of pattern.

*Opposite, below: Anonymous, **The Water Color Class** (detail). Watercolor on paper, 14-5/8 × 23-5/8. America, c. 1815. The Art Institute of Chicago. Gift of Emily Crane Chadbourne.*

Women who enrolled in painting and drawing academies at the end of the 18th century did not aspire to careers as professional artists, but were content to rank their painting skill among other polite accomplishments. This watercolor may record a class at Robertson's Columbia Academy of Painting, a school that operated in New York City from 1792 until about 1821.

The highest technical achievement of a well-trained young lady was the needlework picture, a delicately worked piece of silk embroidery usually based on a contemporary engraving of a biblical or mythological scene. Although needlework pictures were not uncommon during the second half of the eighteenth century, it was during the early years of the Republic that they flourished. Placing the stitches properly required patience and skill and needlework pictures often took several terms to complete. The painted pictures that were done by schoolgirls often bear a close kinship to embroidered pictures, particularly in the lack of attention to perspective and the rendering of forms in space, and it is likely that embroidery designs rather than models from nature were often the inspiration in their painting classes.

The parents who paid to have their daughters educated as ladies did so to assure that they would have the training and polite manners necessary to attract the attentions of young gentlemen. The increasing wealth in America at the close of the eighteenth century permitted men to select wives who would bring large dowries to the marriage and had the ladylike polish necessary to play a role in society. It was no longer necessary that they be trained to run the family business or even to take charge of all aspects of housekeeping. Once the trend toward gentility had begun, it proved impossible to reverse. As economic survival became increasingly more difficult for unmarried women, upper-class girls found it ever more essential to attract a wealthy husband. To do so they cultivated the frivolous characteristics of the lady even more assiduously. Moralists who had hoped that accomplished young ladies would continue to practice spinning, cooking, and Bible-reading and would avoid cultivating expensive tastes for extravagant luxuries were unable to persuade Americans to follow their pronouncements. Most accomplished women who could afford the cost strove to become ladies of fashion.

Fashionable Ladies

Most of the accomplishments taught in the ladies' schools took considerable effort to master. To fulfill the ideal of her teachers, the young graduate had to discuss art and literature with wit and charm; she should be able to dance and ought to know how to sing and play a musical instrument in order to entertain company. Relatively few women, however, mastered the social arts. Rebecca Franks complained in 1781 that "few N[ew] York Ladies know how to entertain company in their own houses unless they introduce the card tables....in NY you enter the room with a formal set curtsey and after the how do's 'tis a fine or a bad day & those triffling nothings are finish'd all's a dead & calm 'till the cards are introduc'd when you see pleasure dancing in the Eyes of all the Matron's." Too often the only traces left of a ladies' academy education after a few years was a taste for cards or billiards, the habit of reading novels, and an interest in fashion.

Just as the separate education of upper-class boys and girls was designed to emphasize the differences between the sexes, the clothing styles of the late eighteenth and early nineteenth centuries sought to make ladies look as much unlike gentlemen as was possible. From head to foot the lady of fashion distorted her natural appearance in order to conform to current European standards of aristocratic beauty. Most of these devices were uncomfortable if not actually dangerous to health. Yet the ability to conform to the ideal clearly identified a woman of high social status and set her off from those poorer women whose clothing was merely practical.

To be in fashion ladies began the distortion of the appearance with their heads. The hair fashion in vogue on the eve of the American Revolution was the towering pompadour headdress that originated in the court of Marie Antoinette. To create the necessary elevation, women's hair was frizzed and stretched over a cushion or rolls called Talemontagues, which were stuffed with a variety of unsavory materials, including cow tails, straw, hay, horsehair, wool, and old hair removed from wigs. The finished structure was treated with pomatum or powder to keep it stiff. These "heads" took hours to complete, so women left them intact for long periods—sometimes several weeks. Naturally, they attracted an even wider variety of vermin and insect life than the simple hair styles of the poor and middle-class women, which could be brushed fairly clean. American ladies' headdresses became lower after the Revolution, and toward the end of the century shorter styles imitative of classical statues became popular along with curly wigs.

Above: **18th-century Wig Curler with Clay Curling Pins.** *Colonial Williamsburg Foundation, Williamsburg, Va. (Photo: Peggy Barnett)*

In colonial America the torturous demands of prevailing hair styles often made women turn to wigs or false curls for society dress. The early 19th century, however, saw a rage for ladies' wigs, and fashionable women hastened to adopt the short curly-headed look of the classical Empire style. In 1800 young Eliza Southgate wrote to her mother begging $5.00 for a false headpiece. "Now, Mama," she coaxed, "I must either cut my hair or have one . . . for nobody has long hair." Some extremists shaved their heads and wore wigs continuously.

John Durand (attrib.), **Mrs. Lewis Burwell.** *Oil on canvas, 37 × 29 in. Virginia, c. 1770. Virginia Historical Society, Richmond.*

Musical accomplishment was considered a social virtue among upper-class women in colonial America. The aristocratic Lucy Randolph Burwell of "Kingsmill," James City County, is shown here playing a popular stringed instrument of the period.

Opposite Anonymous, **Hey Day! is this my Daughter Ann?** *Hand-colored engraving, 22-3/8 × 17-1/2 in. framed. London, June 14, 1774. Cora Ginsburg. (Photo: Peggy Barnett)*

Hair styles during the second half of the 18th century caused a furor both at home and abroad. The principal offender was the towering pompadour headdress popular during the 1760s and 1770s, which was adopted in a limited way by Americans bent on showing their awareness of current European fashions. The proper Quaker Elizabeth Drinker noted in her Philadelphia diary for July 4, 1778: "A very high head-dress was exhibited through the streets this afternoon on a very dirty woman, with a mob after her with drums, etc., by way of ridiculing that very foolish fashion."

Calash. *Silk and bone, 18-11/16 × 20-9/32 in. America, late 18th century. Philadelphia Museum of Art. (Photo: Will Brown)*

One of the most popular bonnets worn in Revolutionary America was the calash, which was constructed perfectly to cover large headdresses.

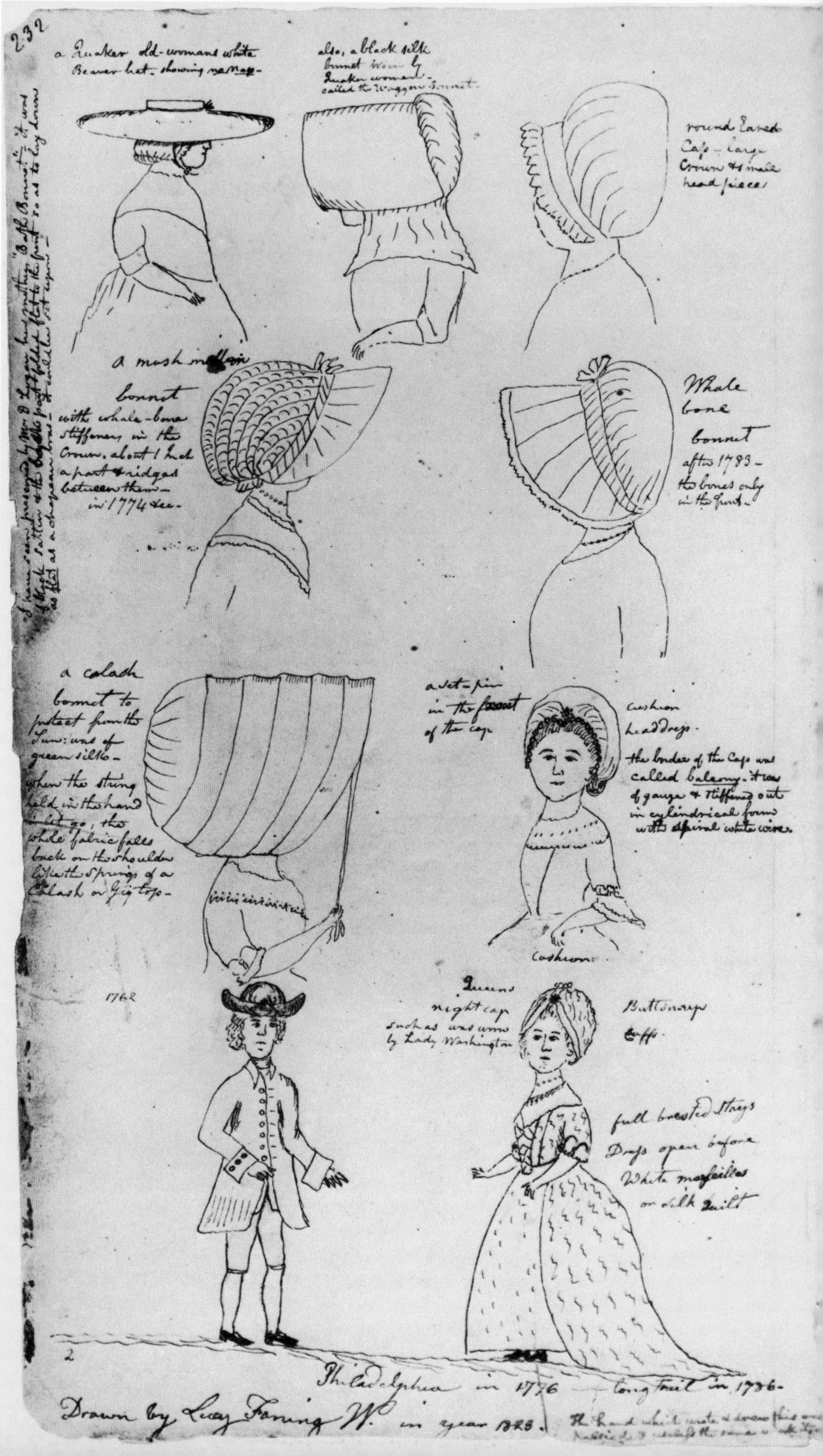

114

a Quaker old-womans white Beaver hat showing no nap—

also, a black silk bonnet worn by Quaker woman called the Waggon Bonnet.

round Eared Cap—large Crown & small head pieces

a mush muslin bonnet with whale-bone stiffeners in the Crown, about 1 Inch apart & ridged between them in 1774 &c—

Whale bone bonnet after 1783— the bones only in the front—

a colash bonnet to protect from the Sun: was of green silk— when the string held in the hand in taking off, the whole fabric falls back on the shoulders like the springs of a Calash or Gig top—

1762

a set-pin in the forepart of the cap

Cushion head dress. the border of the Cap was called Balcony. it was of gauze & stiffened out in cylindrical form with several white wires

Cushion

Queens night cap such as was worn by Lady Washington

Buttonup Cuffs

full breasted Stays Dress open before White marseilles or silk quilt

2

Philadelphia in 1776— long tail in 1776—

Drawn by Lucy Fanning W. in year 1823.

*Left: Lucy Faning Watson, **Ladies' Dresses.** Pen on paper, 13-1/8 × 7-3/16 in. Philadelphia, 1823. Historical Society of Pennsylvania, Philadelphia. (Photo: Joseph Kelley)*

*Opposite: Lucy Faning Watson, **Caps and Bonnets.** Pen on paper, 13-1/8 × 7-3/16 in. Philadelphia, 1823. Historical Society of Pennsylvania, Philadelphia. (Photo: Joseph Kelley)*

*While preparing his voluminous **Annals of Philadelphia, or Facts Illustrative of the History of the City of Philadelphia,** John Faning Watson called on his 70-year-old mother to pen sketches of ladies' fashions worn in Revolutionary America. The variety of caps and bonnets shown here are only a few of the wide assortment available to 18th-century ladies, who generally covered their heads both indoors and out.*

Right: Rufus Hathaway (attrib.),
Sylvia Church Weston Sampson. *Oil on canvas, 37-1/2 × 25-1/4 in. Duxbury, Massachusetts, 1793. Private collection. (Photo: Ron Jennings)*

Most colonial Americans looked on bathing as a dangerous and unhealthy practice. Although colonists washed in spots with lye soap, few except Indians and African slaves were inclined to plunge entirely into water. Indian women scented themselves with sweet grasses, fish oil, and even skunk oil. Upper-class Americans took refuge in a variety of perfumes to disguise natural scents, and fashionable ladies like Sylvia Sampson (1768-1836) sometimes made a virtue of necessity and added delicate perfume bottles to their retinue of elegant accessories.

Opposite, above:
Alexander S. Gordon, **Box, possibly a Patch Box.** *Silver, 3/4 × 1-1/2 × 1 in. New York, 1795–1803. Museum of the City of New York. Gift of Mrs. Charles E. Atwood.*

Both men and women of fashion wore tiny patches – usually on the face and neck – from the 17th century until the beginning of the 19th. Cut in fanciful heart and animal shapes, these delicate "beauty marks" were often stored in little enamel or silver boxes.

Opposite, below:
M. Buchoz, M.D., **The Toilet of Flora.** *…6-7/8 × 4-3/8 in. London, 1772. Library Company of Philadelphia. (Photo: Joseph Kelley)*

Although the use of cosmetics was never as extensive among white women in America as it was in Europe, colonial women were not immune to its attractions. Indian women painted their faces and tattooed their bodies in symbols and individual patterns. Dolley Madison was said to have used rouge and somehow lived to the age of 81 with shiny black tresses. This book contained a wealth of beauty secrets for white women.

Hair styles influenced the shape of hats and bonnets, and before the end of the eighteenth century hats were usually large, although little skimmers were in vogue during the reign of the pompadour headdresses and straw hats were worn throughout the year after the 1730s. Some headcovering was considered proper, even indoors, and milliners offered a dizzying array of hats and bonnets, whose styles changed frequently. Lace caps, accordion-shaped silk bonnets known as calashes, and elaborate headdresses ornamented with gauze, feathers, fake jewels, ribbons, and pearls were fashionable, although sometimes subject to ridicule in the press. The *Pennsylvania Gazette* in August 1776 published a letter from a London lady telling her correspondent that:

> the head is drest as high and as broad as it is possible to make it, with two or three yards of different coloured gauze, interspersed with feathers, artificial carrots, radishes and sallad; the whole being at least one yard in height; and I do assure you, strange as it may appear, that I saw a Lady last week, whose cap was curiously ornamented with a *Sow* and *six Pigs.*

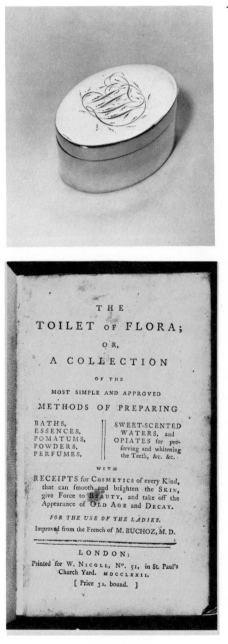

During the 1790s women began dressing their hair in the style of the ancients; one popular cut called for looping a long lock of hair back from the face. Many ladies wore their hair short at the back with long bangs draped over their foreheads, and extremists even sheared off all their hair at the scalp. Women now covered their short curls with turbans or chose from a wide array of bonnets and caps that were available in shops.

Ordinary women used nothing for their complexions except an occasional scrubbing with lye soap, but the face that appeared below a lady's headdress was treated with a variety of cosmetics which, it was hoped, would heighten beauty or delay aging. *The Lady's Magazine,* a London periodical, carried a formula in 1772 for "Balsamic Water to prevent wrinkles"—a precious blend of barley water and balm of Gilead—that had to be shaken for twelve hours to work.

After the middle of the eighteenth century American women also had a variety of jewelry to choose from, including earrings, necklaces, pins, rings, combs, lockets, watch trinkets, and elegant buttons, made of enamel, paste, gilt, or real pearls and other gems. Other accessories included silk stockings, gloves or mitts, fans, umbrellas, and embroidered pocketbooks and, in the early nineteenth century, silk reticules and beaded bags.

Ordinary women wore comfortable clothing, but fashionable ladies, and even little girls, of the second half of the eighteenth century wore tight-bodiced gowns, and bone stays were necessary to give the appearance of a tiny waist. Contemporary newspapers and engravings poked fun at the torturous practice, and one concerned bachelor complained that they offered "scarce any view at all of the Ladies Snowy Bosoms." During the middle of the eighteenth century, skirts were worn full, and women sported large panniers or false hips with metal hoops to support a costly show of heavy material. During the 1780s, hoops were replaced in vogue by pouter-puff bosoms filled out with gauzy buffonts, and false rumps—forerunners of the bustle—to extend the back of skirts. False buffont bosoms led one critic to lament the trend for "a *bosom* two feet and a half in diameter, open work…[with] dark spots, light spots, hills and dales, etc., but no inhabitants…."

Colonial dress styles varied widely; however, the sacque, consisting of a dress or jacket with large box pleats hanging loose from the shoulders at the back, was popular from the 1720s until after the Revolution, although the pleats in back were generally stitched closer to the bodice later in the century. Sacques were worn closed over a full skirt, or open to expose a stomacher. Gowns with close-fitting, pointed bodices were also popular. Many elaborate dresses had matching petticoats, but by mid-century, it was normal to wear a finely quilted petticoat of another material and color. The polonaise, a style popular in the 1780s, called for an overskirt festooned at the sides and back over an exposed petticoat. Women wore sleeves covering the elbow, often trimmed with matching ruffles, and lace or gauze cuffs.

Although the average American woman of the period had to rely on homespun for clothing, the upper classes showed a decided preference for silk. After the middle of the century, ladies preferred brightly printed chintzes for everyday wear. The period between 1750 and 1815 was distinguished by a universal decolletage in dress. Eighteenth-century ladies might cover their shoulders with lace or gauze fichus, while their early nineteenth-century counterparts turned to long shawls to protect bare arms.

The 1790s brought a revolution in feminine fashions, largely a product of the classical revival sweeping Europe at the time. Simultaneously, the number of young ladies seeking to follow European modes increased, and the high-waisted, narrow lines of the Empire style replaced the earlier full skirts and tight stays. Although older women might still need to corset themselves if they tried to follow the new style, young ladies went without lacing. Indeed, since the desired effect was one of bareness with diaphanous white muslin clinging in the manner of classical sculpture, ladies had to abandon all but the briefest underclothing. In the spring of 1801 a Georgia newspaper sarcastically offered to award a prize "To the lady…who shall so arrange her few garments as to appear nearest to naked." The style that appeared merely ludicrous on warm days in the American South could be deadly when worn, as it was, during New England winters. In November 1801 the *Connecticut Courant* carried a cautionary verse, which began:

> Plump and rose was my face
> And graceful was my form,
> Till fashion deem'd it a disgrace
> To keep my body warm.

Riding habits and other outdoor clothing were cut in the prevailing European mode, and in the eighteenth century habits were quite masculine in style, with collars and buttons like those on contemporary men's coats. After the turn of the century they were adapted to reflect the high-waisted feminine styles then in vogue.

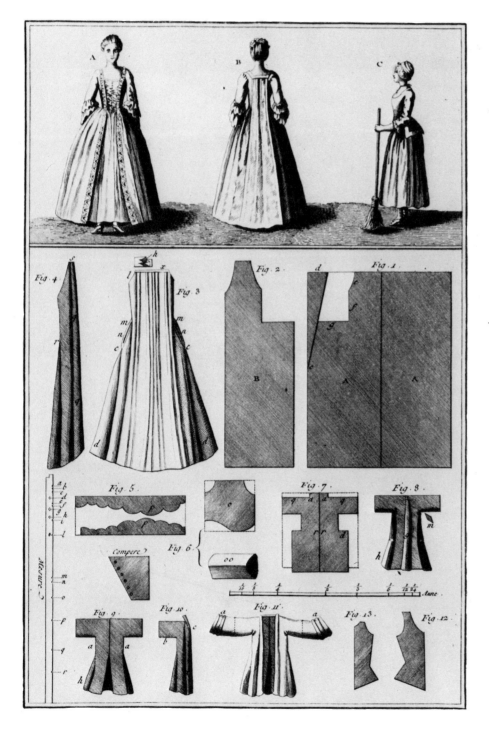

Left: Anonymous, **Couturiere.** Engraving, 15-1/4 × 9-3/4 in. France, 1777. Colonial Williamsburg Foundation, Williamsburg, Va.

American dressmakers turned to engraved fashion plates and patterns from abroad for their dress designs. This example is Plate 117 in **Suite de Recueil de Planches, sur les Sciences, les Arts Libéraux et les Arts Méchaniques avec leur Explication.**

Opposite, above: **Lady's Gown.** Cotton on white muslin. New England, 1800–10. Plymouth Antiquarian Society, Mass. (Photo: Peggy Barnett)

The short-sleeved, high-waisted, narrow lines of the classical Empire style favored diaphanous muslins, often woven with silver and gold threads, designed to cling in the manner of ancient sculpture. Worn with a filmy chemise and little or no support, these skimpy gowns led one critic to bemoan the "transparent depravity" then affecting the fair sex.

Opposite, center: **Sacque Robe, with Matching Petticoat and Stomacher.** Ribbed silk with china silk trim, linen lining. Maryland, 1766–74. Maryland Historical Society, Baltimore. (Photo: Peggy Barnett)

This elegant gown is said to have belonged to Bridget Goldsborough Singleton (1744–74) of Talbot County, Maryland, who died nine months after her wedding to John Singleton in 1774. Although the sleeves have been shortened, the over-all lines of the gown are in keeping with the cut of later sacques.

Opposite, below: **Lady's Cardinal.** Wool and silk. New York, late 18th century. Cora Ginsburg. (Photo: Peggy Barnett)

Most colonial women wore cloaks for outdoor clothing, and red wool cloaks, called cardinals, were popular from the 17th century to the 19th. Other common outer garments were capuchins, short silk or satin cloaks, and Josephs, similar to overcoats and popular during the mid-18th century. The Artois, a variation on the Joseph with additional capes, was favored during the 1790s. This cardinal has a vest sewn inside it for warmth.

Left: Elizabeth Shurtlef, **Pocketbook.** Wool on canvas worked in Irish stitch, 3 × 7 in. Plymouth, Massachusetts, 1740–90. Plymouth Antiquarian Society, Mass. (Photo: Peggy Barnett)

During the 18th century both men and women frequently carried pocketbooks to hold miscellaneous currency, coins, and documents. Although leather was by far the most popular material used, embroidered pocketbooks worked in wool on canvas enjoyed a vogue in America between 1740 and 1790. These colorful accessories were stitched primarily by women for family and friends or for themselves. Many incorporate the date and the name or initials of the owner or maker.

Below: E. M. Brevuort, **Beaded Bag.** Beads on linen, silk lining, 8-1/4 × 6-1/4 in. America, c. 1810. Alvin and Davida Deutsch. (Photo: Peggy Barnett)

During the Republican era ladies' reticules and beaded bags replaced the leather or embroidered pocketbooks popular in the 18th century. This elaborate bag is unusual in design in that it depicts a contemporary naval officer standing near his ship.

Opposite: **Fan.** Ivory, mother-of-pearl, satin, brass, and watercolor, 10-1/2 × 17-1/2 in. Probably made in China for the American market, 1800–25. The Litchfield Historical Society, Conn.

Opposite, left:/18th-century lady's shoe. Pilgrim Antiquarian Society, Plymouth, Mass. (Photo: Peggy Barnett)

The soles of men's and ladies' shoes were cut without any differentiation for the shape of feet, with most women's shoes of the 18th century little more than 3-1/2 inches in width. This slipper belonged to Mercy Otis Warren.

Opposite, below: **Pattens.** *Leather, iron, replacement hide strings, 2-3/8 × 8-1/2 × 2-3/4 in. Pennsylvania, 1760–90. Chester County Historical Society, West Chester, Pa. (Photo: Peggy Barnett)*

Right: After John Collet, **Tight Lacing, or Fashion before Ease.** *Mezzotint, 16 × 11-1/2 in. London, c. 1770. American Antiquarian Society, Worcester, Mass.*

Aristocratic women wore bone stays throughout the second half of the 18th century, when dress styles required the appearance of a tiny waist. This popular English print satirizes the torturous practice, which threatened the health of many fashion-conscious women.

Opposite, right: **Stays.** *Linen and bone, 15-1/2 × 16 in., closed. New England, 1770–85. Plymouth Antiquarian Society, Mass. (Photo: Peggy Barnett)*

Shoes worn by ladies contrasted sharply with the heavy leather footwear worn by ordinary women. Lightweight, thin-soled slippers with high heels and pointed toes were fashioned for ladies of silk brocade and embroidered satins up to the end of the eighteenth century. A lady, these shoes said, never walks through a barnyard or through garbage- and manure-strewn streets. She spends her days in carpeted drawing rooms or rides to visit her friends in a coach. With the advent of the classical Empire style, high heels were replaced by flat-soled slippers or sandals, which were somewhat easier to walk in but still impractical. Since American ladies could not be carried everywhere they went, it was sometimes necessary for them to cope with rain, snow, mud, and filthy streets. Rather than don a pair of sensible leather shoes as worn by the lower classes, ladies often wore pattens, a type of overshoe raised on a metal frame. These were a bit tricky to balance, but a young lady maneuvering through the streets of Philadelphia in a pair of pattens for the first time said she "trotted along quite comfortable, crossing some streets with the greatest ease...."

The waste and frivolity represented by ladies of fashion were condemned by American moralists from the moment large numbers of Americans began to ape the style of European aristocrats shortly after the middle of the eighteenth century. Although Americans had always emulated Europeans, there was not sufficient wealth to reproduce the more expensive styles until the last third of the century. A book by Anthony Benezet entitled *Some Serious and Awful Considerations, recommended to All, particularly the Youth...*, which was published in Philadelphia in 1769, criticized the new-fashioned education being given to upper-class girls. "It is much to be lamented," he wrote, "that our daughters, whose right education is of the utmost importance to human life, should not only be brought up in pride, but in the lowest and most contemptible part of it; such as a fondness for their persons, a desire of beauty, and a love of dress; and indeed almost every thing they meet with seems to conspire to make them think of little else." Before the Revolution the need to economize and avoid the use of imported English luxuries in order to support the patriot boycott of taxed goods, helped to restrain upper-class women somewhat. Even those loyalists who might have been tempted to continue their consumption of English goods found that shopkeepers refused to stock them for fear of provoking a patriot mob. But when the war was over, the number of fashionable ladies increased.

The dignified, serious, independent, and hard-working upper-class matrons of an earlier age soon disappeared. At the dawn of the nineteenth century, wealthy young girls saw clearly that their beauty rather than their strength or ability was the quality most necessary for success. "Wisdom says it is a fading flower," young Molly Tilghman of Maryland wrote to her cousin, "but fading as it is, it attracts more admiration than wit, goodness, or anything else in the world." Only lower-class women preserved the older virtues, which soon came to be identified as "masculine."

Opposite: John Singleton Copley, **Mary MacIntosh and Elizabeth Royall.** *Oil on canvas, 57-1/2 × 48 in. Boston, c. 1758. Museum of Fine Arts, Boston. Julia Knight Fox Fund.*

In Revolutionary America upper-class children were dressed like miniature adults as soon as they had passed infancy, and some girls' rich silk and satin gowns vied with those of their mothers in elegance.

Creative Women

In the eighteenth and nineteenth centuries women generally expressed their creativity by ornamenting items they produced for the use of their families, and by keeping private diaries or writing letters to friends. A few women, however, in the fields of art, literature and the performing arts, managed to attain a certain degree of public recognition.

The first American of either sex to become a professional sculptor was Patience Lovell Wright. Born in Bordentown, New Jersey, she is said to have begun her career modeling bread dough for the amusement of her children. When she was widowed in 1769, Wright moved her family to New York City, where she opened a waxworks. Her sister Rachel Wells assisted her, and by 1772 they had created a traveling exhibit of a new kind. Earlier sculptors in wax had produced doll-like representations of historical or allegorical characters, but Wright took models from life and reproduced their features so accurately that they appeared real. She herself had a forceful personality, talked constantly, and spoke to her models—who were some of the most important people in English and American society—as equals, sprinkling her conversation with profanity. Generally her manner was considered amusing rather than offensive, and she was able to go to London with letters of introduction from leading figures in America. Her career prospered, and she was soon sending advice to the king and queen addressed to them as "George" and "Charlotte." She enjoyed politics and participated in diplomatic intrigues during the Revolution. Combining flamboyant showmanship with her natural talent, Patience Wright was able to support herself through her art. She, however, was exceptional. No other American woman is known to have made a living entirely through painting or sculpture between 1750 and 1815.

The earliest known American woman artist was Henrietta Johnson (or Johnston), who died in 1729 in Charleston, South Carolina. She drew pastel portraits, some of which survive. Almost a century passed before the nieces of Charles Willson Peale—Anna Claypoole Peale and Sarah Miriam Peale—were elected as academicians to the Pennsylvania Academy of the Fine Arts, the first women to receive this honor. Sarah Peale, who painted in oils, is generally considered to be the first professional American woman painter. Other early female painters of repute, such as the miniaturists Anna Peale, Sarah Goodridge, and Ann Hall, also did most of their work after 1815. Thus, the surviving record of paintings done by women in the intervening years consists largely of schoolgirl drawings.

Opportunities for women to receive training in painting and drawing were limited. Classes in these subjects were offered at female seminaries and, beginning in about 1800, instruction also was available in art academies. Those women who were unable to study at a girls' school or drawing academy could learn from contemporary painting manuals and often used engravings for the source of their designs.

A few women in the post-Revolutionary decades were fortunate enough to study with professional artists. Hetty Benbridge studied miniature painting in Philadelphia with Charles Willson Peale, and Hannah Crowninshield of Salem, Massachusetts, took lessons from the artist Michel Felice Corné and painted watercolors in that city before her marriage in 1819. Other women who studied with artists were Sarah Perkins, Ellen Wallace Sharples, and Anna Maria von Phul. Among the untrained artists, Eunice Pinney of Connecticut did not begin to paint until she was almost forty and took her subject matter from contemporary engravings and woodcuts in eighteenth-century children's books. Mary Ann Willson, who lived with her female companion in Greene County, New York, sold primitive watercolors to local farmers as rare "works of art." Finally, in an age before cameras, wealthy ladies touring America, such as the Baroness Hyde de Neuville, might make watercolors or drawings of local sights and even botanical sketches in order to have a record of their trip. These are valuable historical documents.

Many women wrote and quite a few women published poetry in the late eighteenth and early nineteenth centuries. The foremost woman poet was Sarah Wentworth Apthorp Morton, who used the pen names *Constantia* and *Philenia*. Born to a prosperous Massachusetts family, she had a good education and read extensively. Her husband, Perez Morton, was a politically prominent lawyer. Sarah Morton began to write poetry when still a young girl, but she was thirty before her first piece was published in the *Massachusetts Magazine*. Her first long poem, *Ouabi: or The Virtues of Nature*, an American Indian tale in four parts, was published in 1790. In the introduction she asked the reader to "make many allowances for the various imperfections of the work, from a consideration of my sex and my situation; the one by education incident to weakness, the other from duty devoted to domestic avocations." In the introduction to another work published several years later, her defensiveness reflects the increasing restrictions on activity considered "proper" for ladies: "I know, my fair friends, that with many who do not write, application to literature in a female is imagined to imply a neglect of appropriate duties. As this idea has originated rather in misapprehension than malignity, it may not be improper to observe, that it is only amid the leisure and retirement, to which the sultry season is devoted, that I permit myself to hold converse with the Muses; nor does their enchantment ever allure me from one personal occupation, which my station renders obligatory...."

Versatile Susanna Haswell Rowson, who was America's first best-selling novelist, was forced by economic hardship to earn money with her many talents. Although she was raised in the aristocratic circle in Boston, her loyalist father lost his property during the Revolution, and the man she married in 1787 was a poor businessman. Her best-known novel, *Charlotte Temple*, which was published in 1791, was a popular hit and went through more than two hundred editions. The plot is a standard seduction melodrama: an English schoolgirl is carried off to New York by an English army officer who then deserts her. After the heroine's death her seducer is punished for his villainy by agonies of remorse. Despite the contrived plot and wooden characters, the book appealed

Hetty Benbridge (attrib.), **John Poage.** *Watercolor on ivory, gold, and glass, 2-1/8 × 1-9/16 in. Charleston, South Carolina, c. 1773. Greenfield Village and Henry Ford Museum, Dearborn, Mich.*

Only a few miniatures have been attributed to this obscure painter who studied with Charles Willson Peale in Philadelphia before her marriage to the artist Henry Benbridge about 1772. This painting was probably done in Charleston soon after Hetty joined her husband there in 1773; she is believed to have died about a year after her arrival.

Below: Patience Wright, **Lord Chatham (William Pitt, the Elder).** *Clothed wax figure, life size. London, completed 1779. Westminster Abbey, London.*

The only figure known to survive from the hand of the "Promethian modeler" Patience Lovell Wright (1725–86).

Far right : Anonymous, **Mrs. Wright.** *Engraving (8-5/32 × 5-1/16 in.) from the* **London Magazine,** *December 1, 1775. The Library of Congress, Washington, D.C.*

Patience Wright's lifelike figures were applauded in London as a "new style of picturing superior to statuary and peculiar to herself and the honour of America." Relying on her recollection of the subject, the eccentric Patience would model a wax head on her lap while "her strong mind poured forth an uninterrupted torrent of wild thought, and anecdotes and reminiscences of men and events."

MᴿˢWRIGHT.

Publish'd as the Act directs Decʳ 1. 1775.

130

Eunice Pinney, **Charlotte's Visit to the Vicar.** Watercolor on paper, 13-1/2 × 9-3/4 in. Connecticut, 1810. Colonel Edgar William and Bernice Chrysler Garbisch.

Nearly fifty paintings survive from the hand of Eunice Griswold Pinney (1770–1849) a mother of five from Connecticut. Like other untrained artists of the period, she often relied on contemporary engravings for her design sources, and though her watercolors are amateurish in their use of perspective and the rendering of volumes in space, their lively patterns and orderly composition give them a well-deserved place in the history of American naive painting.

CHARLOTTES VISIT to the VICAR.

The good old man was sitting upon his bench at the sight of Charlotte he forgot his ole age and his oaken stick and ventured to walk towards her She ran to him and made him sit down again. Eunice Pinneys Drawing. 1810

Far left: Ellen Wallace Sharples (attrib.), **Mrs. John Bard.** *Pastel on paper, 9-1/8 × 7 in. America, 1793–1801. National Gallery of Art, Washington, D.C. Gift of Louise Alida Livingston.*

Born probably in Birmingham, England, Ellen Wallace (1769–1849) studied painting and drawing with the artist James Sharples at Bath before becoming his third wife in 1787. In 1793 the Sharpleses came to America and took commissions in various American cities, including Philadelphia and New York, during which period Ellen, who had studied drawing as "an ornamental art for amusement," decided to turn professional as a copyist of her husband's works. After returning to England in 1801, they came back to America in 1809, where they remained until James died two years later.

Left: Sarah Perkins, **Mrs. Caleb Perkins.** *Pastel on paper, 25 × 21 in. Plainfield, Connecticut, 1790–99. The Connecticut Historical Society, Hartford.*

Sarah Perkins (1771–1831) was a young amateur pastelist who did a group of portraits, mostly of her family, during the 1790s. Her limited palette gives a two-dimensional quality to her work, yet the portraits show an attempt at modeling that indicates some training in art. A possible teacher was Joseph Steward, who worked in nearby Hampton before 1790 and also did pastels.

Barbara Schultz (attrib.), **Schwenkfelder Birth Certificate of Lydia Kriebel** *(born 1786). Watercolor and ink on paper, 16 × 13 in. Pennsylvania, 1806. Private collection.*

Like other German Protestant religious groups, the American Schwenkfelders practiced the art of manuscript illumination. Sarah Reinwald, Sarah Jaskel, Salome and Hannah Kriebel, and Susanna Hübner are some of their known female artists. This birth and baptismal certificate is attributed to Barbara Schultz on the basis of a signed example in the Schwenkfelder Library, Pennsylvania.

Dante Militaire des Sauvages devant Le President T. Monroe 1821

Baroness Hyde de Neuville
(attrib.), **Indian War Dance.** *Watercolor,
pencil, and ink on paper, 7-5/8 × 12 in.
Washington, D.C., 1821. Abby Aldrich
Rockefeller Folk Art Collection,
Williamsburg, Va.*

*This sketch records a performance during a
visit of a delegation of Pawnee, Omaha,
Kansa, Oto, and Missouri tribes to President
Monroe in Washington on November 29,
1821. Some of the recognizable figures are
Eagle of Delight (the woman sitting in the
group to the left), Generous Chief (in
feathered headdress, lower left),
Chou-man-i-case (heron headdress in center),
and President Monroe in the background. The
central figure in long coat and tricorn near the
President may be the husband of the artist.*

Anna Maria von Phul (attrib.), **Creole
Woman and Boy.** *Watercolor on paper, 9-7/8
× 7-3/4 in. St. Louis, Missouri, c. 1818.
Missouri Historical Society, St. Louis.*

*A little-known woman painter of the early
19th century, Anna Maria von Phul
(1786–1823) was a watercolorist who
painted in Lexington, Kentucky, and St.
Louis, having studied painting and drawing
with the artists George and Mary Beck, who
opened a school in Lexington in about 1800.
Both the von Phul family and the Kentucky
artist Matthew Harris Jouett (who painted her
portrait) encouraged her to pursue her artistic
interests.*

Right: Baroness Hyde de Neuville (attrib.), **Scrubwoman.** *Watercolor and ink on paper, 7-1/2 × 6-1/2 in. New York, 1807–1809. The New-York Historical Society.*

Married to the Bourbon supporter the Baron Hyde de Neuville, Anne-Marguerite-Henriette-Rouille de Marigny (1779?–1849) made two extended visits to the United States, living here in exile between 1806 and 1814, and again, when the Baron was the French Minister, between 1816 and 1822. She made a large number of sketches depicting significant events, important buildings, and occurrences from everyday life in the new Republic.

costume de Scrobeuse, d'après Jone nièce de Martha church

Right: Mary Ann Willson (attrib.), **Nuestra Senora demonte Carmel** *(Our Lady of Mount Carmel). Watercolor and ink on paper, 12-1/8 × 9-11/16 in. Greene County, New York, 1800–25. Museum of Fine Arts, Boston. M. and M. Karolik Collection.*

Little is known about the life of Mary Ann Willson, an apparently untrained artist who settled in Greene County about 1800 with her female companion, Miss Brundage. Evidence suggests that the two women "formed a romantic attachment" for each other (the modern homosexual novel **Patience and Sara** *is based on their lives); in any case, they lived quietly and without criticism, Miss Brundage farming and keeping house while Mary Ann painted primitive watercolors using pigments made from store paint, berries, and brick dust. She received up to 25¢ for these "rare works of art," which a contemporary admirer testified were sold from "Canada to Mobile."*

Opposite: Mary Ann Willson (attrib.), **The Leave Taking.** *Watercolor and ink on paper, 13-11/16 × 10-11/16 in. Greene County, New York, 1800–25. Museum of Fine Arts, Boston. M. and M. Karolik Collection.*

Margaret Mitchell, **Garden Lilly.** *Watercolor and ink on paper, 8 × 6-5/8 in. Medford, Massachusetts (?), c. 1800. New Hampshire Historical Society, Concord. (Photo: Finney)*

This charming watercolor was done at Mrs. Rowson's Academy.

Right, above: Words by Susanna Haswell Rowson, **National Song…4th of July.** *Printed sheet music. Boston, 1818. American Antiquarian Society, Worcester, Mass.*

to popular tastes. In addition to *Charlotte Temple*, Rowson published a number of other novels, worked as a governess, ran her own school, and for five years was on the stage. She was not particularly talented as an actress, but she had a pleasing personality and could dance, sing, play both harpsichord and guitar, compose lyrics, and write plays. Her most successful stage production was an operetta entitled *Slaves in Algiers, or a Struggle for Freedom.* A popular musical farce called *The Volunteers* was based on the Whiskey Rebellion. Her last stage appearance was in a three-act comedy of her own composition, *Americans in England, or Lessons for Daughters.*

High-quality dramatic performances did not begin in America until the middle of the eighteenth century when a company of professional performers from England made its debut in Williamsburg. The company was led by Mr. and Mrs. Lewis Hallam, and the *Virginia Gazette* praised the "scenes, Cloaths, and Decorations entirely new, extremely rich, and finished in the highest Taste." The American Company, as it later came to be called, toured America with a repertoire including Shakespeare and other favorites, such as Gay's *The Beggar's Opera* and Garrick's *Miss in Her Teens.* The players enjoyed great popularity and made repeated appearances in all the major cities from New York to Charleston, and also in some small communities where only the most primitive stage facilities were available. After Lewis Hallam's death, his wife—whose first name is not known—remarried and continued to perform under her new name, Mrs. David Douglass. Her son, Lewis Hallam, Jr., became her leading man. Later stars of the American Company were Nancy Hallam, Maria Storer, and Mary Ann Pownall, who had been known in England as Mrs. Wrighten and who composed songs featured in the company's operas and plays.

S.F.B. Morse (attrib.),
Susanna Haswell Rowson? *Oil on canvas,
30×25 in. America, 1800–25. Worcester Art
Museum, Mass.*

*In addition to being a novelist, playwright,
and actress, Susanna Rowson was also an
academy preceptress who opened a popular
school for young ladies in the Boston area at
the end of the 18th century. She carefully
supervised the progress of her pupils,
published several textbooks, and in 1805
inaugurated the annual exhibitions of
academy projects that were widely acclaimed by
the local press.*

Above: Anonymous, **Mrs. David Douglass** *(Mrs. Lewis Hallam). Watercolor on ivory, glass, and gold, 2-1/2 × 2 in. America, 1756–74. The Walter Hampden–Edwin Booth Theater Collection and Library, New York.*

Mrs. Lewis Hallam was a leading lady of the first major theatrical company in colonial America. She was born in England and was a member, together with her husband, of her brother-in-law's troupe, which came to America in 1752 and toured until 1756, when Lewis Hallam died. Mrs. Hallam then married David Douglass, another actor, who took over the company and renamed it the American Company of Comedians. Mrs. Douglass probably died in Philadelphia in 1774.

R. Dighton Pinx.   R. Laurie Sc.

M.^{rs}   Wrighten.

Pub.^d as the Act Directs March 1.st 1780 by Wm Richardson N.º 68 High Holborn.

Opposite, R. Laurie, after R. Dighton, **Mrs. Wrighten.** *Mezzotint, 8-1/2 × 6 in. London, March 1, 1780. Metropolitan Museum of Art, New York. Harris Brisbane Dick Fund.*

Mary Ann Pownall (1756?–1796), who was well known as Mrs. Wrighten for her "singing chambermaid" roles in London's Drury Lane, came to America in 1792, where she joined the Hallam company at Philadelphia's Southwark Theater. She was later engaged by John Joseph Leger Sellee to perform at Church Street Theater, in Charleston, where she delighted South Carolina audiences from 1795 until her untimely death in 1796.

Gilbert Stuart, **Sarah Wentworth Apthorp Morton.** *Oil on canvas, 29-1/4 × 24 in. Philadelphia, 1802. Museum of Fine Arts, Boston. Julia Cheney Edwards Collection.*

Sarah Morton, leading woman poet of her generation, was born in Boston to a wealthy family and grew up in the cultured, politically active societies of Boston and Braintree. Her home in Dorchester, where she moved in 1797, was a salon frequented by other writers and distinguished Americans of the day. She was a great beauty (Stuart painted three portraits of her), but her life was not joyful. Boston was scandalized by the affair between her husband and her sister Frances, who later committed suicide, and she suffered "stagnation of heart" over the death of her only son and one of her four daughters.

Far better known than Sarah Morton is the Boston poet Phillis Wheatley. She attracted widespread attention in both America and England during her lifetime both because of her precocity—her first poem was published while she was still in her teens—and because of her race. Phillis Wheatley was a first-generation African slave. When she was brought to Boston as a small child, just losing her baby teeth, she spoke no English. But she was naturally bright, and her owners took pleasure in teaching her to speak, to read, and to write. The daughter of the family even taught her Latin. Since very few blacks in early America had such educational opportunities, Phillis Wheatley's achievements were displayed as evidence of the intellectual capacities of blacks. Education, religion, and virtue were common themes in her writing; the neoclassical influence of Alexander Pope can be seen in these lines from a piece entitled "To the University of Cambridge Wrote in 1767":

> While an intrinsic ardor bids me write,
> The muse doth promise to assist my pen
> 'Twas but e'er now I left my native shore
> The sable land of error's darkest night.
> There, sacred Nine! for you no place was found
> Parent of mercy, 'twas the powerful hand
> Brought me in safety from the dark abode.

She was freed after her owner's death, was deserted by the free black man she married, and ended her life in poverty, working as a domestic in a boarding house. She died at about the age of thirty-one, and her best poem, "Liberty and Peace," was published posthumously.

*Above: Phillis Wheatley, **America**. Autograph manuscript poem, 11-3/4 × 7-5/16 in. Boston, 1770–80. The Library Company of Philadelphia. (Photo: Joseph Kelley)*

*Right: Southwark Theater, **For the Benefit of Miss Storer**. Playbill 8-1/2 × 5-3/4 in., Philadelphia, 1770. Historical Society of Pennsylvania, Philadelphia. (Photo: Joseph Kelley)*

*Theater companies frequently held performances for the benefit of their players. Miss Storer was one of four sisters who acted with the American Company of Comedians; this performance featured Steele's **Tender Husband**.*

Anonymous, **Phillis Wheatley, Negro Servant to Mr. John Wheatley, of Boston.** *Engraving, 6-1/2 × 4-3/8 in. London, September 1, 1773. New York Public Library. This engaging portrait of Phillis Wheatley (1753?–1784), the young black poet, appeared as the frontispiece to her only published book,* **Poems on Various Subjects, Religious and Moral.**

Presidents' Ladies

During the Revolution and the Confederation period, there was no American chief of state. Although the Continental Congress had a presiding officer, he had little authority. When the new federal government was established under the Constitution in 1789, many Americans hoped that the new executive officer would become a symbol of American nationhood by assuming some of the attributes of royalty that had been lost when the United States repudiated King George III. With the exception of widower Thomas Jefferson, who had stern views on the subject of republican simplicity, the early Presidents all attempted to establish a social atmosphere during their administrations comparable to that maintained by the ruling classes in European nations. As they attempted to reproduce as best they could the polished, sophisticated atmosphere of European capitals, their wives became the models for what an upper-class American lady should be like. Martha Washington, Abigail Adams, and Dolley Madison were queens of a republican court.

Martha Washington had the greatest difficulty of the three in fitting into the role of republican queen. She had been born in 1731 and was nearly sixty when she became "Lady Washington," as she was called during her husband's presidency. She had never been to Europe, much less to court. She was plump and had for years not attempted even the Virginia reel, which was the usual dance for Chesapeake people in the days of her youth. She had not been to a dancing school, and so she simply sat and watched while her husband took other partners for the quadrilles and minuets. Nor had she been educated in any accomplishments other than needlework. She had not read widely, she had slight interest in politics, and she could not make sparkling conversation. Particularly in comparison with her successor, many people thought her rather dull.

The life Martha Washington preferred was that of plantation mistress. After the death of her first husband, she inherited a large estate, and with her marriage to George Washington took over the management of his household at Mount Vernon. During his absence she was in charge of all plantation affairs. But Washington missed her when he was away, and during the war she stayed with him at camp every winter. She had hoped that once the war was over "we should be suffered to grow old together, in solitude and tranquility," but when her husband was chosen President she resigned herself to leaving Mount Vernon and taking up the social demands of President's wife. However, she never enjoyed them. She wrote to a relative in Virginia, "I live a very dull life here... indeed I think I am more like a state prisoner than anything else...there is certain bounds set for me which I must not depart from—and as I can not *due* as I like I am obstinate and stay at home a great deal," and in another letter noted the irony of the situation in which she "who had much rather be at home, should occupy a place with which a great many younger and gayer women would be extremely pleased."

The social responsibilities of the first President's wife included presiding at state dinners on Thursdays and at "drawing-room" receptions every Friday. All "respectable" persons were admitted to these receptions without special invitation, but formal dress was required and rules of protocol were carefully observed. If any lady but the Vice-President's wife attempted to move into the spot at Mrs. Washington's right hand, the President himself would intervene to rec-

An Acc.t of Mrs Washington's Expences from Virginia to my Winter Quarters & back again to Virginia according to the Mem.ms and acc.ts which I have received from her & those who accomp.d her.

		Lawful		
1775 Dec.r 1776. July.	To amount of her Exp.s from Virginia to Cambridge	85	2	6
	To Ditto from New York to Virginia after the Enemy landed on Staten Island. Including her Residence in Philadelp.a at Board for sometime — p.r acc.t	180	2	8
1777 Mar.r	To Ditto from Virginia to Morris Town While the Troops lay there in Wint.r	61	10	—
May.	To Ditto from Morris Town to Virg.a including a few days stay in Philadelp.a	74	—	—
1778 Feb.r	To Ditto from Virg.a to Valley forge	52	8	6
June	To Ditto from Valley forge back to Virg.a when the Army took the Field	54	—	—
Dec.r	To Ditto. to Phil.a where she was at the request of Congress	48	—	—
1779 June	To Ditto back to Virginia from Middleb.k when the Army marched from its Cantonments at that place	72	—	—
Dec.r	To Ditto in coming to Morristown when the Army was Cantoned in the vicinity of it	63	5	—
1780 June	To Ditto on her return to Virginia from that place	68	—	—
Nov.r	To Ditto. her Expences to my Quar.rs at New Windsor	78	6	8
June 1781	To Ditto back to Virginia from thence, when the army took the field — Including a few days stay in Philad.a	85	—	—
July 1782	To her Expences from Newburgh to Virginia	72	—	—
Dec.r	To Ditto from Virginia to Newburgh	70	5	8
		£1064	1	—

Errors Excepted

July 1.st 1783

G.o Washington

*Right: Martha Washington, **Seat Cushion** (one of a set). Worsted and silk on canvas, 3 × 18-3/4 × 15-1/2 in. Virginia, New York, or Philadelphia, 1766–1802. Mount Vernon Ladies' Association, Mount Vernon, Va. (Photo: Peggy Barnett)*

Like many 18th-century ladies, Martha Washington was an accomplished needlewoman; indeed, from the number of textiles worked by her that survive, it would seem that she often took refuge in her embroidery. The seat cushion shown here is part of a set that she worked over a period of thirty years, beginning in 1766, in a classic shell pattern using a simple cross-stitch. In 1799 a visitor to Mount Vernon noted that the furnishings in the sitting parlor included "yellow bottomed windsor chairs."

Below: Trunk used by Martha Washington during the Revolution. Mount Vernon Ladies' Association, Mount Vernon, Va. (Photo: Peggy Barnett)

*Opposite: George Washington, **An account of Mrs. Washington's Expenses from Virginia to my Winter Quarters and back again during the Revolutionary War.** ... autograph manuscript. July 1, 1783. Mount Vernon Ladies' Association, Mount Vernon, Va.*

Undoubtedly the most prominent camp follower of the American Revolution, Martha Washington repeatedly joined her husband at his winter quarters during the war. Several months before he resigned his commission in 1783, Washington submitted a list of her expenses totaling $1064 to Congress for reimbursement.

Dinner Plate. *Hand-painted porcelain,*
1 × 9-3/4 in. Sèvres, France, 1784.
Smithsonian Institution, Washington, D.C.

After the Revolution many leading Americans
developed a taste for French furniture and
accessories. Although the Washingtons never
ventured abroad, their furnishings at Mount
Vernon included French porcelains and a
lady's desk for Martha, and the Madisons, too,
adorned their Virginia estate with imported
china and furniture. Jefferson's French
furniture for Monticello is well known, and
this Sèvres plate was part of a set bought
abroad by Abigail and John Adams between
1783 and 1785.

Gilbert Stuart, **Mrs. John Adams.** *Oil on*
canvas, 29 × 23-3/4 in. Boston, 1815.
National Gallery of Art, Washington, D.C.
Gift of Robert Homons.

tify the situation. Although these affairs were far more relaxed than the receptions held by European royalty, they could hardly be called informal. Martha Washington was relieved when the days of formal visits in the state coach and ceremonial dinners were over. After her return to Mount Vernon she reported herself "steady as a clock, busy as a bee, and cheerful as a cricket." But while she had not enjoyed the Presidential society, she believed it was important to maintain it. In one of her rare public comments on political affairs, she startled a group of visiting Federalists by making some "pointed and sometimes very sarcastic" remarks about "the new order of things" established by Thomas Jefferson.

Abigail Adams, who was Vice-President's lady as well as President's lady in the early days of the republican court, was Martha Washington's partner in many of the social occasions in the capital cities of New York and Philadelphia. She would be seated on Martha Washington's right at the weekly Friday evening reception. Abigail Adams had had far better training for such ceremonies than Martha Washington, having spent the years from 1783 to 1788 in Europe where her husband served in various diplomatic missions. She had inspected the European courts and mixed in diplomatic society at The Hague, London, and Paris. Her head was not turned by court life—she told Thomas Jefferson that she preferred her Braintree farm to "the court of St James's where I seldom meet with characters so innofensive as my Hens and chickings, or minds so well improved as my garden"—but she certainly understood it. And she agreed that some pomp was needed in a republic.

Abigail Adams was widely read, and although she was not "accomplished"—she could not speak French very well, her handwriting was not elegant, and her spelling was highly original—she could discuss art and literature far better than most Americans. In addition she had a most unladylike passion for politics. Whereas Martha Washington might be known as "Lady Washington," Abigail Adams was known as "Mrs. President." She had strong opinions on every issue of the day and did not hesitate to express them. Some men believed that she, not President Adams, was making the administration policy. Certainly her position of chief adviser to the President was more important than her social role during the years when she was President's lady.

In the early years of the republic the government was located in New York and Philadelphia, cities with some claim to sophistication. In 1800, however, the capital moved to the Potomac. For the last few months of her husband's term as President, Abigail Adams was the first mistress of what was then known as the President's House in Washington, D.C., which was situated in what was little more than a barren swamp. (Abigail Adams even got lost in the woods trying to find her way to Washington from Baltimore.) The President's House was not completed, and it was all Abigail Adams could do to make it livable. She was too busy trying to dry out the house, find enough firewood to last through the winter and a place to hang her washing to have much time for social life. She observed that "this House is built for ages to come. The establishment necessary is a task which cannot be born by the present sallery." When the ladies from Georgetown came to pay their respects to the President's wife, she dutifully returned the calls, but these events were by no means comparable to the "court" affairs of Philadelphia. "Yesterday," she wrote to her sister, "I returned fifteen

Opposite **Gown** *worn by Dolley Madison. Silk velvet with silver trim. America (?), 1800–15. Greensboro Historical Museum, N.C. (Photo: Bradford Rauschenberg)*

Dolley Madison's love of elegant fashions has left her the reputation of being one of the best-dressed women in the early history of the White House. A sentimental woman, she kept this gown until her death.

John Vanderlyn (attrib.) after Gilbert Stuart, **Mrs. James Madison.** *Oil on canvas, framed, 35 × 30 in. America, c. 1830–50. Greensboro Historical Museum, N.C. (Photo: Bradford Rauschenberg)*

Dolley Madison enjoyed extraordinary popularity during most of her long life; nearly all historians agree that the gregarious wife of the "great little Madison" was the single most dominant force in the social life of the early Republic.

visits—but such a place as Georgetown!...It is the very dirtyest Hole I ever saw for a place of any trade or respectability of inhabitants. It is only one mile from me, but a quagmire after every rain."

It was left to the lively Dolley Madison to establish a republican court in Washington. As wife of the Secretary of State, she became the social leader of the new capital city during the presidency of Thomas Jefferson. Both Jefferson and Vice-President Aaron Burr were widowers and the President had no inclination to emulate the "aristocratic" practices of Europeans in his entertaining. Once he even chose to receive a British diplomat attired in formal court dress while he himself wore a dressing gown and shabby slippers. Many people, including Martha Washington and Abigail Adams, thought that Jefferson carried his notion of "republican" simplicity too far.

When James Madison became President in 1809, the nation finally had a woman in the President's House for whom society was a chief interest. Despite her restricted Quaker upbringing, Dolley Madison showed a flair for high fashion and gracious entertaining that had a strong impact on social life in the Federal City. She was not a particularly handsome woman—an English official described her as "fat and forty but not fair"—but her love of elegant gowns and turbans made her a favorite model for American ladies to copy. A determined shopper, Dolley Madison's letters to France ordering the latest fashions constitute a notable part of her surviving correspondence, and in one order the duties alone amounted to two thousand dollars.

Working with the architect and designer Benjamin Henry Latrobe, the First Lady decorated the President's House in the style of the English Regency and inaugurated the legendary Wednesday night "drawing rooms" and frequent state dinners that attracted adherents of all political persuasions. Although these entertainments attended more closely to protocol than the informal gatherings of the Jefferson administration, everyone agreed that Dolley Madison was a relaxed and charming hostess who never let politics interfere to spoil social occasions. Representative Jonathan Roberts wrote, "By her deportment in her own house you cannot discover who is [sic] her husband's friends or foes."

When the British captured Washington in 1814 and burned the public buildings, Dolley Madison remained alone in the President's House until the last possible moment. Later, in a letter to Mrs. Benjamin Latrobe, she confided, "I confess that I was so unfeminine as to be free from fear, and willing to remain in the *Castle*. If I could have had a cannon through every window, but alas! those who would have placed them there, fled before me..." Before abandoning the building to the British, Dolley Madison salvaged a few treasures including a portrait of George Washington and some important state papers. After the fire, the Madisons returned to Washington to temporary presidential quarters. There, Dolley Madison resumed her former gracious entertaining. When her husband's term expired and the couple was about to depart to their home in Virginia, the citizens of Georgetown gave a ball in Mrs. Madison's honor. They summarized their gratitude to this queen of the republican court in a bit of verse:

A charming WOMAN, still we find,
Like the bright SUN, cheers all Mankind,
And like it, is admired by all!

Liberty and Equality

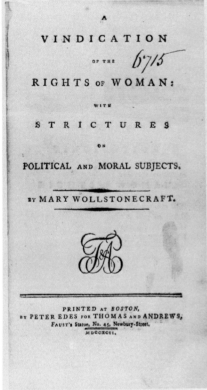

Opposite: Thacara & Vallance, Engraved frontispiece from **The Lady's Magazine and Repository of Entertaining Knowledge.** *8-1/2 × 5-3/16 in. Vol. I. Philadelphia, December 1, 1792. The Library Company of Philadelphia. (Photo: Joseph Kelley)*

This engraving graced the initial number of a new magazine for female readers, imitative of a long-established English periodical with a nearly identical title. In a probable allusion to Mary Wollstonecraft's **Vindication of the Rights of Woman,** *this allegorical image depicts Woman presenting a petition entitled "Rights of Woman" to the seated figure of Liberty. The magazine included excerpts from the Wollstonecraft book.*

Mary Wollstonecraft, **A Vindication of the Rights of Woman: with Strictures on Political and Moral Subjects.** *Boston, 1792. The Library Company of Philadelphia. (Photo: Joseph Kelley)*

The egalitarian principles of the Declaration of Independence had obvious implications for women. But in the decades following the Revolution they came into conflict with the code of ladylike behavior which emphasized the differences between the sexes. As upper-class women strove to demonstrate they were as good as European women of the "better sort," they grew less independent and their status relative to men declined. At the same time, provisions of the English common law that restricted the rights of women were interpreted and enforced more strictly than in the past.

This repressive legal phase developed gradually and, because of the primitive state of American courts before the Revolution, many of the laws that would have limited the freedom of American women were ignored. Thus women were theoretically forbidden to appear in court if they were married, yet they appeared anyway. Although married women had no legal right to any of their property, one may read notices such as the following in American newspapers: "I, Sarah Smith, School-mistress, the wife of William Smith, take this method to inform the public not to trust or credit the said Smith on my account, for I shall never pay any of his contractions.... I nine years have been his wife, tho' he for a widower doth pass, when he meets a suitable lass; for his wicked doings I never more can him abide, nor he never more shall lie by my side."

In eighteenth-century America men and women not uncommonly made formal agreements between themselves to get around the provisions of the law. Examples include both prenuptial and postnuptial property agreements. In February 1770 Robert Bartlett and Jane Spooner signed a contract in which the former relinquished all right to his intended bride's real or personal estate "for the future good and advantage of the said Jane and in testimony of the good will and affection, which the said Robert hath for the said Jane." Once married, a woman could not sign such an agreement, but the husband might make a unilateral statement such as that signed by John Fordery Edmonds of Plymouth, in which he agreed "to let Elizabeth Edmonds my wife to have the sole Disposal of all those Goods, Estate Real and Personal Bequeath'd by Her late Husband." If a husband did not sign such a document permitting his wife to retain control of her property, courts and other legal authorities would enforce the law.

Men and women might even negotiate their own divorce agreements. The following typical item appeared in a Virginia newspaper in 1774: "COLEMAN THEEDS and ELIZABETH, his Wife having this Day parted by mutual Consent, and given Bond each to the other, the Subscribers being Witnesses to their Agreement, that they will not interfere with any Estate which shall hereafter accrue to either Party, this Notice is given to the Gazette, that no Person, after this Date, may credit the Wife on the Husband's Account, or the Husband upon that of the Wife's." Remarriage might follow such a separation, although no legal authority had authorized the divorce.

*Susan Sedgwick, **Elizabeth Freeman** (Mumbet). Watercolor on ivory, 4-1/2 × 3-3/4 in. Massachusetts, 1811. Courtesy Massachusetts Historical Society, Boston. (Photo courtesy National Portrait Gallery, Smithsonian Institution, Washington, D.C.)*

*Opposite: Anonymous, **On Bryan Sheehen**...Broadside, 15-5/16 × 10-5/32 in. Salem, Mass., January 16, 1772. Courtesy Massachusetts Historical Society, Boston. (Photo: George M. Cushing)*

Under colonial law, men convicted of rape were subject to the death penalty. This broadside describes the events leading to the conviction of Bryan Sheehen for the rape of Abial Hollowell, wife of Benjamin Hollowell of Marblehead. Sheehen pleaded not guilty, contending that Hollowell was a compliant partner in the act. After one stay of execution he was hanged.

A husband had a right to his wife's body as well as to her property, and during the transitional period in American law, advertisements for runaway wives might run together with divorce agreements. A typical announcement appeared in a South Carolina newspaper: "Whereas my wife, Mary Oxendine, hath eloped from me, this is to forewarn all persons from Harbouring or entertaining her, day or night, or crediting her in my name, as I am determined not to pay any debts by her contracted. All masters of vessels or others, are hereby cautioned against carrying her off the province, as they may expect to be prosecuted with the utmost severity.—She is of fair complexion, with light colour'd hair, and has a mark over one of her eyes."

Women were subject to criminal as well as civil statutes in eighteenth-century America. Like male miscreants, they could be stripped and flogged, branded, or have their ears or noses cropped. Serious crimes, including rape and robbery as well as murder, were punished by death. Not until the nineteenth century did imprisonment become a punishment for crime. Harsh as these penalties were, however, they were milder than those imposed in England. Not only did the English impose the death penalty for a far greater variety of offenses, but they had some particularly grim forms of execution. Under English law, for instance, a woman who murdered her husband was guilty of "pethy treason" and would be burned alive. In America, however, there were virtually no executions by burning except in the case of slaves. Even witches, who were always burned in Europe, had been hanged in America during the Salem witchcraft hysteria at the end of the seventeenth century.

As the law's balance shifted further and further in favor of men's rights over those of women, there was surprisingly little protest. Dissatisfied women most often demanded the right to a serious education. The frivolous accomplishments of ladies were considered insulting to women's intelligence by some and inappropriate in a republic by others. "Is it reasonable," demanded Judith Sargent Murray in an article published in the *Massachusetts Magazine*, "that...an intelligent being...should at present be so degraded, as to be allowed no other ideas, than those which are suggested by the mechanism of a pudding, or the sewing of the seams of a garment?"

Yet one searches in vain for criticism of the patriarchal family or appeals by women for political rights. Their most extreme demand would appear to have been that of Abigail Adams in her "Remember the Ladies" letter, to modify the English common law formulations that gave husbands unlimited power over wives. In 1792 Mary Wollstonecraft's book *Vindication of the Rights of Woman* became available in the bookstores of Boston and Philadelphia. The only part of this English feminist's work that appeared to attract much attention at this time was the portion decrying fashionable education for women on the grounds that it led women "shamefully to neglect the duties of life." The book became popular in girls' schools, but its readers were not inspired to agitate for increased legal or political rights.

On BRYAN SHEEHEN,

A Criminal this Day executed in Salem, for committing, in the most cruel and shocking Manner, a RAPE on the Body of Abial Hollowell Wife of Benjamin Hollowell, of Marblehead.

January 16, 1772.

UNHAPPY Man, your Race is just compleat;
And God your righteous Judge you soon must meet.
Raging with cruel Lust, the Laws you've broke:
O now prepare to meet the awful Stroke!

Your wicked Life, how lustful, how obscene!
Pregnant with Guilt, and ev'ry Act unclean.
Full in the Path of Wickedness you've trod,
Despis'd a Saviour, and profan'd your God.

A Thought on Christ you never could bestow,
But vainly hop'd his Laws to overthrow.
To whore and drink has been your mighty Aim:
Lying——Swearing——compleats your wretched Name.

Hardened in Sin, and prone to ev'ry Crime
You, O Sheehen, must die before your Time.
Repent, O Man, implore redeeming Love,
To gain Admission to the Realms above.

The gathering Crowd proclaims the fatal Day:
Sheehen come forth—you Justice must obey.
The Cart prepar'd, your Coffin in it see;
And all compleat t' approach the dismal Tree.

In View of Death, with Thousands gath'ring round,
The solemn March can't but your Soul confound.
The hardest Heart must now your case bemoan,
And thank his God—your state is not his own.

The Gallows see—all hope of Life is o'er,
And soon, O very soon, you'll be no more.
Call on your God, his Mercy humbly crave,
And cry to Jesus Christ, your Soul to save.

At length, O sad, you reach the awful Place,
While ev'ry Heart bewails your shocking Case.
Now fervently God's faithful Servants pray,
That your poor Soul with Christ may be this Day.

You mount the Cart, and on your Coffin stand,
A sorrowful Warning to all the Land.
May all who see the Havock Sin has made,
Bless the great God for his restraining Aid.

See Sheehen now upon the Brink of Death,
And in a Moment must resign his Breath.
Over his Face you see the Cap now falls,
While he to God most high for Mercy calls.

Justice commands——see the Cart is started,
And from his Body * his Soul is parted;
And plunging into the eternal World,
To Heav'n or Hell his Soul is quickly hurl'd.——
* Just before he was turn'd off, (which was precisely at Half past Three o'Clock,) he desired his Body might be given to Dr. Kast of Salem for dissection.

Printed and Sold opposite the Prison in Queen-street; at which Place, may be had his Life and Character.

Nevertheless, the feminist implications of the Declaration of Independence did not go completely unnoticed. Without any recorded discussion of the subject, the Constitution of the State of New Jersey adopted in 1776 and later state election laws confirmed the right of property-owning women (widows and spinsters) to vote in state elections. A loophole in the common law, which extended the franchise to the few unmarried women who owned large amounts of property, existed throughout the colonial period, but very few women exercised the right to vote even when they qualified. Few New Jersey women voted under the new state constitution until the political parties that developed in the 1790s began to employ the votes of women—including young girls and married women who were clearly ineligible—as a way of assuring election victory. As a matter of "election reform" New Jersey disfranchised women in 1807. But for a short time that state had followed the principle requiring consent of the governed in a free society to a logical conclusion.

Black women, who were almost always slaves and owned no property, were even less likely than white women to draw feminist conclusions from the principles of the American Revolution. For slaves of both sexes, liberty meant freedom from a master and equality meant self-respect. Black women as well as men took advantage of the disorder created by the war to seize their freedom, and both followed the white men's armies—British as well as American—hoping their service would earn them emancipation. Many white Americans became sensitive to the injustice of slavery for the first time while fighting for their own liberty, and after the Revolution one northern state after another abolished the institution.

In Massachusetts Elizabeth Freeman, usually known as Mumbet, earned an important place in history when she successfully sued for her freedom. Although she was not educated, she had learned "by keepin' still and mindin' things" that the law said all people were born free and equal. Once free, she went to work as a paid servant in the home of the lawyer who had taken her case to court. The family for which she worked obviously admired and respected her, and she was well enough paid to be able to buy a house of her own where she lived with a daughter in her old age.

Elizabeth Freeman had asserted that slavery contradicted the lofty principles of the Revolution. But neither she nor any other woman of her time perceived these principles as promising full equality to the female sex. It would have been surprising if any woman had. Caring for their homes and families, nursing the sick and dying, participating in the political, economic, religious, and cultural activities of their communities, early American women of all races and classes must impress us with their dedicated pursuit of their highest ideals. At a time when mere survival could not be taken for granted, women not only survived but improved the quality of life for themselves and those around them. In the mid-nineteenth century, the abolition and women's rights movements burgeoned simultaneously. Women reformers recalled anew the ringing words of the Declaration of Independence and carried on the legacy of the Revolutionary age.

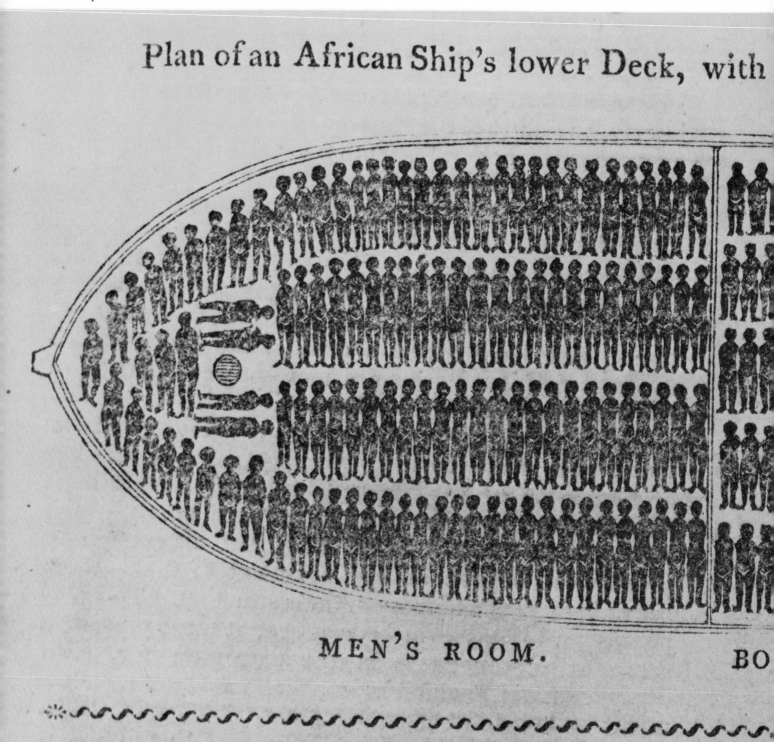

Plan of an African Ship's lower Deck, with

MEN'S ROOM.   BO

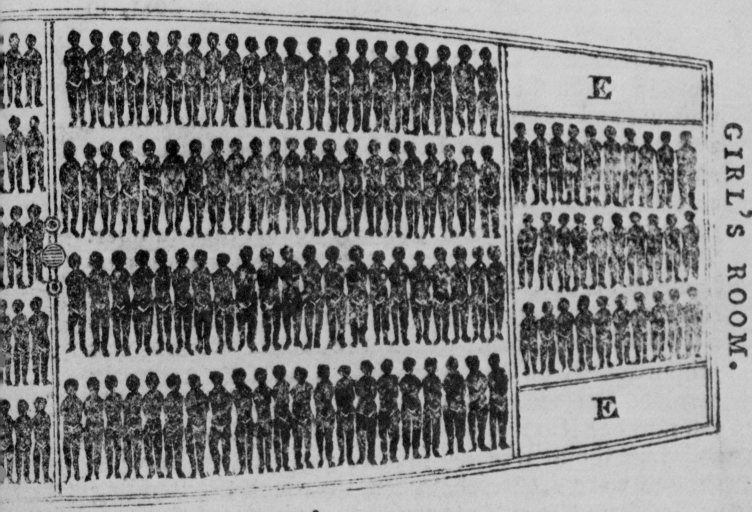

GIRL'S ROOM.

OM.   WOMEN'S ROOM.

Bibliography

These are the principal published sources we consulted while preparing both the exhibition and this book. Of equal importance for our research, though not listed here, were magazines and newspapers read by Americans of the Revolutionary generation, and manuscripts, including women's letters, journals, and other documents.

GENERAL

Benson, Mary Sumner. **Women in Eighteenth Century America.** N.Y., 1935.

De Pauw, Linda Grant. **Founding Mothers: Women of America in the Revolutionary Era.** Boston, 1975.

Earle, Alice Morse. **Colonial Dames and Good Wives.** Boston, 1895.

Evans, Elizabeth. **Weathering the Storm: Women of the American Revolution.** N.Y., 1975.

James, Edward T., James, Janet W., and Boyer, Paul S., eds. **Notable American Women 1607-1950: A Biographical Dictionary.** Cambridge, Mass., 1966.

Leonard, Eugenie Andruss. **The Dear-Bought Heritage.** Phila., 1965.

– – –. Drinker, S., and Holden, M. **The American Woman in Colonial and Revolutionary Times, 1565-1800: A Syllabus with Bibliography.** Phila., 1962.

Spruill, Julia Cherry. **Women's Life and Work in the Southern Colonies.** N.Y., 1972.

LOVE AND MARRIAGE

Blackstone, Sir William. **Commentaries on the Laws of England.** Phila., 1771.

Butterfield, Lyman H. **Adams Family Correspondence.** Cambridge, Mass., 1973.

– – –. **Letters of Benjamin Rush.** Princeton, N.J., 1951.

Calhoun, Arthur W. **A Social History of the American Family from Colonial Times to the Present.** N.Y., 1961.

Chastellux, Marquis de. **Travels in North America.** Chapel Hill, N.C., 1963.

Cott, Nancy F. "Divorce and the Changing Status of Women in Eighteenth-Century Massachusetts." **William and Mary Quarterly,** Oct. 1976.

Genovese, Eugene D. **Roll, Jordan, Roll: The World the Slaves Made.** N.Y., 1974.

Howard, G. E. **A History of Matrimonial Institutions.** N.Y., 1964.

Keyssar, Alexander. "Widowhood in Eighteenth-Century Massachusetts: A Problem in the History of the Family." **Perspectives in American History,** 8, 1974.

Morgan, Edmund S. **Virginians at Home: Family Life in the Eighteenth Century.** Charlottesville, Va., 1963.

Morris, Richard B. "Women's Rights in Early American Law." **Studies in the History of American Law.** N.Y., 1964.

O'Meara, Walter. **Daughters of the Country: The Women of the Fur Traders and Mountain Men.** N.Y., 1968.

Seaver, James E. **A Narrative of the Life of Mrs. Mary Jemison.** Gloucester, Mass., 1961.

Southgate, Eliza. **A Girl's Life Eighty Years Ago.** N.Y., 1887.

MOTHERHOOD

Ariès, Philippe. **Centuries of Childhood: A Social History of Family Life.** N.Y., 1962.

Bremner, Robert H., ed. **Children and Youth in America.** Cambridge, Mass., 1970.

Buchan, William, M.D. **Advise to Mothers.** Phila., 1804.

Cadogan, William, M.D. **An Essay Upon Nursing and the Management of Children, from their Birth to Three Years of Age.** Phila., 1773.

De Mause, Lloyd, ed. **The History of Childhood.** N.Y., 1975.

Earle, Alice Morse. **Child Life in Colonial Days.** N.Y., 1899.

Himes, Norman E. **Medical History of Contraception.** N.Y., 1970.

Hurd-Mead, Kate, M.D. **A History of Women in Medicine.** Haddam, Conn., 1938.

Millspaugh, Charles S. **Medicinal Plants.** Phila., 1892.

Smellie, William, M.D. **An Abridgement of the Practice of Midwifery.** Boston, 1786.

Smith, Daniel Scott, and Hundus, Michael S. "Premarital Pregnancy in America, 1640-1971: An Overview and Interpretation." **The Journal of Interdisciplinary History,** 5, Spring 1975.

Speare, Elizabeth George. **Child Life in New England, 1790-1840.** Sturbridge, Mass., 1958.

Stearns, John. "Account of the Pulvis Parturiens, a Remedy for Quickening Childbirth." **Medical Repository.** N.Y., 1808.

Welch, d'Alte. **A Bibliography of American Children's Books Printed Prior to 1821.** Worcester, Mass., 1972.

SICKNESS AND DEATH

Duffy, John. **Epidemics in Colonial America.** Baton Rouge, La., 1953.

Forbes, Harriette. **Gravestones of Early New England.** Boston, 1927.

Jacobs, G. Walker. **Stranger Stop and Cast an Eye.** Brattleboro, Vt., 1972-73.

Massachusetts Historical Society. **Portraits of Women 1700-1825.** Boston, 1954.

Shryock, Richard H., M.D. "Women in American Medicine." **Journal of American Women's Medical Association,** 5, 1950.

– – –. **Medicine and Society in America: 1660-1860.** Ithaca, N.Y., 1960.

DOMESTICITY

Bishop, Robert. **New Discoveries in American Quilts.** N.Y., 1975.

Bradfield, Nancy. **Costume in Detail: Women's Dress 1730-1930.** Boston, 1968.

Carter, Susannah. **The Frugal Housewife, or Complete Woman Cook.** N.Y., 1792.

Cummings, Abbott Lowell. **Bed Hangings.** Boston, 1961.

Duane, William, ed. **Extracts from the Diary of Christopher Marshall, 1774-1781.** Albany, 1877.

Earle, Alice Morse. **Home Life in Colonial Days.** N.Y., 1908.

– – –. **Two Centuries of Costume in America 1620-1820.** N.Y., 1970.

Fennelly, Catherine. **Food, Drink, and Recipes of Early New England.** Sturbridge, Mass., 1963.

– – –. **Textiles in New England 1790-1840.** Sturbridge, Mass., 1961.

Gridley, Marion E. **The Indian Woman.** N.Y., 1974.

Montgomery, Florence. **Printed Textiles, English and American Cottons and Linens 1700-1850.** N.Y., 1970.

Orlofsky, Patsy and Myron. **Quilts in America.** N.Y., 1974.

Ring, Betty, ed. **Needlework, An Historical Survey.** N.Y., 1975.

Rowe, Ann Pollard. "Crewel Embroidered Bed Hangings in Old and New England." **Boston Museum of Fine Arts Bulletin,** 71, 1973.

Safford, Carleton L., and Bishop, Robert. **America's Quilts and Coverlets.** N.Y., 1974.

Schiffer, Margaret B. **Historical Needlework of Pennsylvania.** N.Y., 1968.

Smith, Eliza. **The Compleat Housewife.** London, 1750.

Tryon, Rolla M. **Household Manufactures in the U.S. 1640-1860.** Chicago, 1917.

Wadsworth Atheneum. **Bed Ruggs 1722-1833.** Hartford, Conn., 1972.

Warwick, E., Pity, Henry, and Wychoff, A. **Early American Dress.** N.Y., 1965.

WOMEN AT WORK

Abbott, Edith. **Women in Industry.** N.Y., 1910.

Blumenthal, Walter Hart. **Brides from Bridewell: Female Felons Sent to Colonial America.** Rutland, Vt., 1962.

Bridenbaugh, Carl. **Cities in Revolt: Urban Life in America, 1743-1776.** N.Y., 1964.

— — —. **The Colonial Craftsman.** N.Y., 1950.

Chudacoff, Nancy F. "Woman in the News 1762-1770—Sarah Updike Goddard." **Rhode Island History,** Nov. 1973.

Davison, Carolina V. "Maximilian and Eliza Godefroy." **Maryland Historical Magazine,** 29, 1934.

Dexter, Elizabeth Anthony. **Colonial Women of Affairs.** N.Y., 1972.

— — —. **Career Women of America, 1776-1840.** Francestown, N.H., 1950.

Fitzpatrick, John C., **The Diaries of George Washington,** III, Boston, 1925.

Miner, Ward L. **William Goddard, Newspaperman.** Durham, N.C., 1962.

Pinckney, Elise, ed., assisted by Marvin R. Zahniser. **The Letterbook of Eliza Lucas Pinckney.** Chapel Hill, N.C., 1972.

Ravenel, Harriott Horry. **Eliza Pinckney.** N.Y., 1896.

Salmon, Lucy. **Domestic Service.** N.Y., 1897.

Smith, Abbot Emerson. **Colonists in Bondage: White Servitude and Convict Labor in America, 1607-1776.** N.Y., 1971.

Wroth, Lawrence C. **A History of Printing in Colonial Maryland, 1686-1776.** Baltimore, 1922.

WOMEN AND RELIGION

Andrews, Edward Deming. **The People Called Shakers.** N.Y., 1963.

Fries, Adelaide L., ed. **Records of the Moravians in North Carolina.** Raleigh, N.C., 1922.

Hoyt, William K. "The Lot, the Youth and the Schobers." **The Three Forks of Muddy Creek,** I, Frances Griffin, ed. Winston-Salem, N.C., 1974.

Jones, Rufus. **The Quakers in the American Colonies.** N.Y., 1966.

Marcus, Jacob R. **The Colonial American Jew, 1492-1776.** Detroit, 1970.

Mason, J. M. **Christian Mourning: A Sermon, occasioned by the Death of Mrs. Isabella Graham.** N.Y., 1814.

Osterweis, Rollin G. **Rebecca Gratz.** N.Y., 1935.

Perrill, John Upton, and Perrill, Donna M. **Indian Women of the Western Morning: Their Life in Early America.** N.Y., 1974.

Tyler, Alice Felt. **Freedom's Ferment.** N.Y., 1962.

Wales, Abby L. **Reminiscences of the Boston Female Asylum.** Boston, 1844.

Wisbey, Herbert A., Jr. **Pioneer Prophetess.** Ithaca, N.Y., 1964.

U.S. Bureau of the Census: **Census of Religious Bodies, 1926.** Government Printing Office, 1928.

WOMEN AT WAR

Blumenthal, Walter Hart. **Women Camp Followers of the American Revolution.** Phila., 1952.

Bruce, Kathleen. **Commonwealth History of Massachusetts,** III, Albert B. Hart, ed. N.Y., 1966.

Commetti, Elizabeth. "Women in the American Revolution." **New England Quarterly,** 20, 1947.

De Pauw, Linda Grant. **Four Traditions: Women of New York in the Era of the American Revolution.** Albany, 1974.

— — —. **Fortunes of War: New Jersey Women and the American Revolution.** Trenton, 1976.

Ellet, Elizabeth. **The Women of the American Revolution.** N.Y., 1969.

Galloway, Grace Growden. **Diary of Grace Growden Galloway.** N.Y., 1970.

Graymont, Barbara. **The Iroquois in the American Revolution.** Syracuse, N.Y., 1972.

Grundy, H. Pearson. "Molly Brant—Loyalist." **Ontario History,** 45, Summer 1953.

Harkness, David J. **Southern Heroines of the American Revolution.** Knoxville, Tenn., 1973.

Kaplan, Sidney. **The Black Presence in the Era of the American Revolution.** N.Y., 1973.

Malone, Henry T. **Cherokees of the Old South.** Athens, Ga., 1956.

Quarles, Benjamin. **The Negro in the American Revolution.** N.Y., 1973.

Reed, William B. **The Life of Esther De Berdt, afterwards Esther Reed, of Pennsylvania.** Phila., 1853.

Robinson, Victor, M.D. **White Caps, The Story of Nursing.** Phila., 1946.

Smith, Samuel Steele. **A Molly Pitcher Chronology.** Monmouth Beach, N.J., 1972.

Somerville, Mollie. **Women and the American Revolution.** Washington, D.C., 1974.

ACCOMPLISHED WOMEN

Adams, Hannah. **A Memoir of Miss Hannah Adams, Written by Herself.** Boston, 1832.

Bentley, William. **Diary: 1759-1819.** 4 vols. Salem, Mass., 1905-1914.

Bolton, Ethel Stanwood, and Coe, Eva Johnston. **American Samplers.** Princeton, N.J., 1973.

Colden, Cadwallader. **The Letters and Papers of Cadwallader Colden.** New-York Historical Society, **Collections,** 50-56, 67-68, 1917-23, 1934-35.

Cremin, Lawrence A. **American Education: The Colonial Experience, 1607-1783.** N.Y., 1970.

Farish, Hunter D., ed. **Journal and Letters of Philip Vickers Fithian, 1773-1774: A Plantation Tutor of the Old Dominion.** Williamsburg, Va., 1945.

Garrett, Elisabeth Donaghy. "American Samplers and Needlework Pictures in the DAR Museum," **The Magazine Antiques**, Feb. 1974; April 1975.

Ginsburg, Cora. "Textiles in the Connecticut Historical Society," **The Magazine Antiques**, April 1975.

Kerber, Linda K. "Daughters of Columbia: Educating Women for the Republic, 1787-1805." **The Hofstadter Aegis: A Memorial,** Elkins, Stanley, and McKitrick, Eric, eds. N.Y., 1974.

Ring, Betty. "The Balch School in Providence, Rhode Island." **The Magazine Antiques,** April 1975.

— — —. "Salem Female Academy," **The Magazine Antiques,** Sept. 1974.

Van Doren, Mark, ed. **Correspondence of Aaron Burr and His Daughter Theodosia.** N.Y., 1929.

Fritz, Jean. **Cast for a Revolution.** Boston, 1972.

Wenhold, Lucy Leinbach. "The Salem Boarding School Between 1802 and 1822." **North Carolina Historical Review,** April 1950.

Woody, Thomas. **A History of Women's Education in the United States.** N.Y., 1966.

FASHIONABLE LADIES
(See the titles on fashion listed under Domesticity)

Tilghman, Molly. "Letters of Molly and Hetty Tilghman, Eighteenth Century Gossip of Two Maryland Girls," J. Hall Pleasants, ed. **Maryland Historical Magazine,** 21.

CREATIVE WOMEN

Andrews, Wayne. "Patience was her Reward: the Records of the Baroness Hyde de Neuville." **Journal of the Archives of American Art,** July 1964.

Bernikow, Louise, ed. **The World Split Open: Four Centuries of Women Poets in England and America, 1552-1950.** N.Y., 1974.

Biddle, Edward, and Fielding, Mantle. **The Life and Works of Thomas Sully.** Charleston, S.C., 1969.

Black, Mary, and Lipman, Jean. **American Folk Painting.** N.Y., 1966.

Bolton, Ethel Stanwood. **American Wax Portraits.** Boston, 1929.

Brandt, Ellen B. **Susanna Haswell Rowson: America's First Best-Selling Novelist.** Chicago, 1976.

Giffen, Jane. "Susanna Rowson and Her Academy." **The Magazine Antiques,** Sept. 1970.

Graham, Shirley. **The Story of Phillis Wheatley.** N.Y., 1949.

Griswold, Rufus W. **Female Poets of America.** Phila., 1859.

Hopkins, Edwin J. **Eighteenth-Century American Arts, the M. and M. Karolik Collection.** Cambridge, Mass., 1941.

Jonas, E. A. **Matthew H. Jouett: Kentucky Portrait Painter.** Louisville, 1938.

Knox, Katherine McCook. **The Sharples: Their Portraits of George Washington and his Contemporaries.** New Haven, 1930.

Lesley, Parker. "Patience Lovell Wright." **Art in America,** 24, Oct. 1936.

Lipman, Jean, and Winchester, Alice. **The Flowering of American Folk Art 1776-1876.** N.Y., 1974.

Little, Nina Fletcher. **The Abby Aldrich Rockefeller Folk Art Collection: A Descriptive Catalogue.** Williamsburg, Va., 1957.

Morgan, John Hill. **Gilbert Stuart and His Pupils.** N.Y., 1969.

Pendleton, Emily, and Ellis, Milton. "The Life and Works of Sarah Wentworth Morton." **University of Maine Studies,** Series 2, 20, Dec. 1931.

Prown, Jules D. **John Singleton Copley—In America 1738-1774,** I. Cambridge, Mass., 1966.

Rankin, Hugh F. **The Theater in Colonial America.** Chapel Hill, N.C., 1965.

Sellers, Charles Coleman. **Charles Willson Peale.** N.Y., 1969.

Stewart, Robert S. **Henry Benbridge (1743-1812): American Portrait Painter.** Washington, D.C., 1971.

Vail, R. W. G. **Susanna H. Rowson, The Author of Charlotte Temple.** Worcester, Mass., 1933.

Van Ravenswaay, Charles. "Anna Maria von Phul." **Missouri Historical Society Bulletin,** 10, April 1954.

Wheatley, Phillis. **Poems and Letters.** Charles F. Heartman, ed. N.Y., 1915.

Willis, Eola. **The Charleston Stage in the Eighteenth Century.** Columbia, S.C., 1924.

PRESIDENTS' LADIES

Anthony, Katharine. **Dolly Madison: Her Life and Times.** N.Y., 1949.

Arnett, Ethel S. **Mrs. James Madison: The Incomparable Dolley.** Greensboro, N.C., 1972.

Klapthor, Margaret B. **Benjamin Latrobe and Dolley Madison Decorate the White House, 1809-1811.** Washington, D.C., 1965.

Smith, Margaret Bayard. **The First Forty Years of Washington Society,** Gaillard Hunt, ed. N.Y., 1906.

Thane, Elswyth. **Washington's Lady.** N.Y., 1972.

LIBERTY AND EQUALITY

Felton, Harold W. **Mumbet: The Story of Elizabeth Freeman.** N.Y., 1970.

Field, Vena Bernadette. "Constantia: A Study of the Life and Works of Judith Sargent Murray 1751-1820." **University of Maine Studies,** Series 2, 17, Feb. 1931.

Flexner, Eleanor. **Mary Wollstonecraft.** N.Y., 1972.

Lurie, Nancy Oestreich. "Indian Women: A Legacy of Freedom." **Look to the Mountain Top,** Robert L. Iacopi, ed. San Jose, Calif., 1972.

Murray, Judith Sargent. **The Gleaner.** Boston, 1798.

Turner, Edward R. "Women's Suffrage in New Jersey: 1790-1807." **Smith College Studies in History,** 1, 1916.

Wardle, Ralph M. **Mary Wollstonecraft: A Critical Biography.** Lincoln, Neb., 1951.

Exhibition Checklist

Entries followed by numbers in parentheses will appear only at some of the museums in the tour of the exhibition as coded below:

1. The Pilgrim Society and The Plymouth Antiquarian Society, Plymouth, Massachusetts.
2. The High Museum of Art, Atlanta, Georgia.
3. The Corcoran Gallery of Art, Washington, D.C.
4. The Chicago Historical Society, Chicago, Illinois.
5. The Lyndon Baines Johnson Library, Austin, Texas.
6. The New-York Historical Society, New York City.

Entries with no numbers following them will appear at all the above museums. An asterisk preceding an entry indicates that the item is illustrated in this book. The following items on the checklist have been deleted from the exhibition: 68, 78, 80, 190, 232.

*1. Anonymous. **Embroidered [wedding?] picture** Wool and silk yarns on linen, 20 1/2" x 14 3/4" (52.1 x 37.5 cm). New England, dated on clock tower "1756." American Antiquarian Society, Worcester, Mass. (1)

*2. Anonymous. **The Old Maid.** Engraving, 10 3/16" x 8 13/16" (30.4 x 22.3 cm). London: Published by J. Walker, November 17, 1777. Library of Congress, Department of Prints and Drawings, Washington, D.C.

3. Anonymous. **A New Bundling Song.** Broadside, 12" x 8 1/2" (30.5 x 21.6 cm). Boston: Printed by Nathaniel Coverly, late 18th century. From the original in the American Antiquarian Society, Worcester, Mass.

*4. Henry Drinker (1734-1809). **Valentine** [to Elizabeth Sandwith (1735-1807)]. Pen and ink, watercolor on cut paper mounted on velvet, 13" (23 cm) in diameter. [Pennsylvania] February 14, 1753. Abby Aldrich Rockefeller Folk Art Collection, Williamsburg, Va.

*5. Anonymous. **Courtship Drawing.** Watercolor and pen on paper, 11 7/8" x 15 1/8" (30.2 x 38.4 cm) framed. Pennsylvania (?), 1800-1825. A North Carolina Collection.

*6. Nat[haniel] Hurd (1729-1777). **Courtship and Marriage.** Engraving, 9" x 8" (22.9 x 20.3 cm). Boston, c. 1760-1775. American Antiquarian Society, Worcester, Mass. (1)

*7. Anonymous. **The Old Plantation.** Watercolor on paper, 16" x 20" (40.6 x 50.8 cm) framed. Found in Columbia, South Carolina, c. 1800. From the original at the Abby Aldrich Rockefeller Folk Art Collection, Williamsburg, Va.

*8. Nicholas Collin (Rector of the Swedish Churches in the State of Pennsylvania). **Marriage Certificate of Robert Jackson and Judith Jones** (free blacks). Printed and completed in manuscript, 7 5/8" x 9 1/4" (19.8 x 23.5 cm). Philadelphia, September 9, 1794. The Historical Society of Pennsylvania, Philadelphia.

9. Anonymous. **Dower chest.** Walnut with maple inlay, 29 1/8" x 53 5/16" x 24 13/32" (74 x 137 x 62 cm). Front feet probably replaced; replacement brasses. Maxatawney Township (?), Berks County, Pennsylvania. inscribed and dated on front "MARIA KUTZ/ 1783." The Philadelphia Museum of Art. (1)

*10. Anonymous. **Dower Chest.** Painted pine, 25" x 37 3/4" x 22 1/2" (63.5 x 95.9 x 57.6 cm). Minor restoration on back feet. Berks County (?) Pennsylvania, c. 1790. Private collection. (2-6)

*11. Anonymous. **Coverlet.** Crewels on linen, 92" x 71" (233.7 x 180.3 cm) including fringe. Pennsylvania, c. 1810. Kate and Joel Kopp, America Hurrah Antiques, New York City.

12. Isaiah Thomas. **Divorce Petition against Mary Thomas.** Manuscript, 12 3/4" x 8" (32.4 x 20.3 cm). Boston, May 27, 1777. From the original at the American Antiquarian Society, Worcester, Mass.

*13. Aristotle (pseudonym). **Aristotle's Complete Master-Piece, in three Parts, Displaying the Secrets of Nature in the Generation of Man....** Printed book, 5 1/2" x 3 3/8" (14 x 8.6 cm). Thirteenth edition. [Philadelphia: Printed by M. Cary] 1796. The Library Company of Philadelphia.

*14. Anonymous. **Maternity dress.** Blue and white striped linen. West Chester, Pennsylvania, c. 1740-1790. Philadelphia Museum of Art.

15. W[illiam] Smellie. **An Abridgement of the Practice of Midwifery: and A set of Anatomical Tables with Explanations.** Printed book, 7 3/4" x 4 3/4" (19.7 x 12.1 cm). Boston: Printed and Sold by J[ohn] Norman [1786]. The Library Company of Philadelphia.

*16. Charles White. **A Treatise on the Management of Pregnant and Lying in Women and the Means of Curing, but more especially of Preventing the principal Disorders to which they are liable.** Printed book, 8 1/2" x 5 1/4" (21.6 x 13.4 cm). Worcester, Massachusetts: Printed by Isaiah Thomas, 1793. The Library Company of Philadelphia.

*17. Anonymous. **Obstetric case with tools.** Wood, brass, leather, steel, wool, 2 1/2" x 18 1/4" x 19 1/2" (6.4 x 46.3 x 49.5 cm) open. Europe, c. 1780. Smithsonian Institution, Washington, D.C.

18. Anonymous. **Obstetrical forceps.** Steel, 16" x 3" (40.6 x 7.6 cm) closed. Eighteenth century (?). Waring Historical Library, Medical University of South Carolina, Charleston.

*19. Joseph Sympson, Jr. (?-1736), after William Hogarth (1679-1764). **A Woman Swearing a Child to a Grave Citizen.** Etching and engraving, 12" x 14" (30.6 x 35.6 cm). London, c. 1730-1735. Anglo-American Art Museum, Louisiana State University, Baton Rouge.

20. Anonymous. **Infant's shirt.** Linen, 7 7/8" x 22" (20 x 58.9 cm). Boston, c. 1764. Collection of Mr. and Mrs. Charles Fox Hovey.

21. Anonymous. **Child's petticoat** (worn by John Wilson). Crewels on homespun wool, 26" (66 cm). Pennsylvania, c. 1760-1780. Chester County Historical Society, West Chester, Pa.

*22. Anonymous. **Child's dress.** Linen embroidered with crewels, 22" x 37" (55.9 x 93.9 cm). America, 18th century. Wadsworth Atheneum, Hartford, Conn. Gift of Mrs. Charles B. Salisbury.

23. Anonymous. **Infant's shoes.** Yellow kid, canvas, China silk, leather, 4 1/2" (11.4 cm). America (?), c. 1805. Textile Resource and Research Center, Valentine Museum, Richmond, Va.

*24. Anonymous. **Child's moccasins.** Deerskin, porcupine quills, dyed deer hair, 5 1/2" x 3 3/4" (13.9 x 9.5 cm). Iroquois, late 18th or early 19th century. Courtesy of the Peabody Museum of Archaeology and Ethnology. Gift of the Misses Palfrey.

25. Anonymous. **Mary P. Dakin.** Oil on wood, 8 1/4" x 6 13/16" (20.9 x 17.3 cm). America, 1811. New York State Historical Association, Cooperstown.

26. Anonymous. **Nipple shield.** Free-blown non-lead glass (impure), 1" x 2 7/8" (2.5 x 7.3 cm) in diameter. New England, c. 1780-1820. Courtesy Society for the Preservation of New England Antiquities, Boston.

*27. John McMullin (1765-1843). **Nipple and tube.** Silver, 7 7/16" (18.9 cm). Mark "I M'MULLIN" (in rectangle flanked by incised star forms, eagle below) above tube. Philadelphia, c. 1795-1800. Museum of Fine Arts, Boston. Gift of Philip L. Spaulding.

28. Thomas Danforth Boardman (1784-1873). **Nursing Bottle.** Pewter, 6 1/2″ (16.5 cm). Marks: (on bottom) "x" in block capital, eagle beneath. "T.D.[B]" the whole within two beaded scrolls; in serrated reverses, "HART-FORD." Hartford, Connecticut, c. 1810-1850. Lent by The Metropolitan Museum of Art. Gift of Joseph France, 1943.

29. Samuel Danforth (1774-1816). **Child's porringer.** Pewter, 1″ x 3 1/8″ (2.5 x 7.9 cm) in diameter. Marks: "S.D" in oval, eagle, sword over "x." Hartford, Connecticut, c. 1795-1816. Mabel Brady Garvan Collection, Yale University Art Gallery, New Haven, Conn.

*30. William Homes (1716/17-1783). **Child's porringer.** Silver, 1 3/4″ x 6 1/8″ (4.6 x 15.6 cm). Mark "HOMES" in rectangle under handle; engraved "I-Q/to/H-Q" on handle. Boston, c. 1740-1770. Museum of Fine Arts, Boston. Bequest of Miss Grace W. Treadwell.

*31. Matthew Harris Jouett (1787/88-1827). **Mrs. Matthew Harris Jouett** (Margaret Henderson Allen, 1795-1873) and **George Payne Jouett** (1813-1862). Oil on wood, 26″ x 20 1/2″ (66 x 52.1 cm). Kentucky, 1814. Collection of Mrs. James Ross Todd.

*32. Henry Inman (1801-1846), after Charles Bird King (1785-1862). **Portrait of a [Chippewa] Squaw and Child.** Oil on canvas, 38″ x 33″ (96.5 x 83.8 cm). America, c. 1830-1840. Courtesy the Peabody Museum of Archaeology and Ethnology, Cambridge, Mass.

*33. "Ehre Vater Artist" [attrib.]. **Birth and Baptismal Certificate of Sarah Zimmerman** [born in Friedland, North Carolina, March 10, 1777]. Watercolor and ink on paper, 15 3/8″ x 12 3/4″ (39.1 x 32.4 cm). Rowan County, North Carolina, c. 1800-1810. Old Salem, Inc., Winston-Salem, N.C.

*34. Anonymous. **The History of Little Fanny, Exemplified in a Series of Figures.** Printed book with cutouts, 4 1/2″ x 3 5/8″ (11.4 x 9.2 cm). Boston: Printed by J. Belcher, 1812. American Antiquarian Society, Worcester, Mass. (1)

35. Anonymous. **ELLEN, or The Naughty Girl Reclaimed, a story, Exemplified in A SERIES OF FIGURES.** Printed book with cutout figures, 5 1/4″ x 4 1/4″ (13.4 x 10.8 cm), in case. Second edition. London: Printed for S. & J. Fuller, 1811. The Colonial Williamsburg Foundation, Williamsburg, Va. (2-6)

*36. Reuben Moulthrop [attrib.] (1763-1814). **Elizabeth and Mary Daggett.** Oil on canvas, 36″ x 28 1/2″ (91.4 x 72.4 cm). Connecticut, c. 1794. The Connecticut Historical Society, Hartford.

*37. Philip Syng, Jr. (1703-1789). **Child's Whistle and Bells.** Silver and mother-of-pearl, 6″ (15.2 cm). Marks "PS" in rectangle, engraved "IH" on whistle. Philadelphia, c. 1750. Museum of Fine Arts, Boston. Bequest of Samuel A. Green.

38. Anonymous. **Doll.** Painted wood, gesso, glass, silk, linen, wool, human hair, 17″ (43.2 cm). England or Germany, late 18th century. The Colonial Williamsburg Foundation, Williamsburg, Va.

39. Anonymous. **Doll.** Carved and painted wood, cloth arms, 10 1/4″ x 2 11/16″ (26 x 6.8 cm). Massachusetts, c. 1790. Collection of the Maryland Historical Society, Baltimore.

*40. Charles Willson Peale (1741-1827). **Rachel Weeping.** Oil on canvas, 36″ x 32″ (91.4 x 81.3 cm) framed. Begun in Annapolis, 1772. The Barra Foundation, Inc., Philadelphia. (2-6)

*41. Anonymous. **Bleeding kit.** Wood, polished steel, pewter, brass, 1″ x 9 1/2″ x 16 1/2″ (2.5 x 24.1 x 41.9 cm) open. European, c. 1780. Smithsonian Institution, Washington, D.C.

42. W. & N. Hutchinson. **Scarifier** (bleeder). Steel and brass, 2 9/16″ x 2 1/8″ x 1 27/32″ (6.5 x 5.4 x 4.7 cm), Sheffield [England], c. 1760-1780. The Charleston Museum Collection, S.C.

43. Anonymous. **Bleeding bowl.** Pewter, 2 1/2″ x 5″ (6.4 x 12.7 cm) in diameter. America, c. 1800. Smithsonian Institution, Washington, D.C.

*44. R. Havell after Geo[rge] Walker. **Leech Finders.** Hand-colored lithograph, 14″ x 18″ (35.6 x 45.7 cm) framed. London: Published by Robinson & Son, April 1, 1814. From the original in the Smithsonian Institution, Washington, D.C.

45. Anonymous. **Medical kit.** Walnut, pewter, glass, iron, brass, 6 1/4″ x 6 1/2″ x 6 1/4″ (15.8 x 16.5 x 15.8 cm). European, c. 1750. Smithsonian Institution, Washington, D.C.

46. William Meyrick, surgeon. **The NEW FAMILY HERBAL; or DOMESTIC PHYSICIAN:...** Printed book, 8 3/16″ x 5 1/4″ (20.8 x 13.4 cm). Birmingham [England]: Printed by Thomas Pearson...and Sold by R. Baldwin, 1790. The Library Company of Philadelphia.

*47. Nathaniel Smibert (?) (1735-1756). **Mrs. George Davies** (Mary Mirick 1635-1752). Oil on canvas, 13″ x 9 1/4″ (33 x 23.5 cm). Massachusetts, c. 1750. Courtesy Massachusetts Historical Society, Boston. (1)

48. Anonymous. **Senility (invalid's) cradle.** White pine, oak, 30 1/2″ x 38 1/2″ x 83 1/2″ (77.5 x 97.8 x 212 cm). America, c. 1832. Schenectady County Historical Society, N.Y.

49. Anonymous. **Memorial ring.** Gold, black and white enamel, watercolor on ivory, glass, 1 3/8″ x 11/16″ (3.5 x 1.8 cm). Inscribed on black enamel "IN DEATH LAMENTED AS IN LIFE BELOVED"; on tomb "WEEP/NOT/FOR/THE/DEAD"; on reverse engraved in script "ELLEN/APPLETON/obt 4 Augt/1791/Aet. 46." England (?), c. 1791-1795. Museum of the City of New York.

*50. Anonymous. **Mourning brooch.** Watercolor on ivory; gold, pearls, glass, 2 1/4″ x 1 5/8″ x 3/16″ (5.7 x 4.1 x .5 cm). Inscribed "Our darling Babe to Heaven has flown and left us in a World of pain" "FCB [Frances Courtenay Baylor, 1779-1780] April 3, 1780." English (?), c. 1780-1785. The Colonial Williamsburg Foundation, Williamsburg, Va. (1)

51. Anonymous. **Sacred to the/memory/of Miss/Clarissa Champion/OB October 22/1801/ AE 16 years 7/months 22 days.** Miniature. Watercolor on ivory; hair, gold, glass, 2 1/2″ x 3 1/4″ (6.4 x 8.3 cm). Initials "CC" on urn. America (?) c. 1801-1805. The Litchfield Historical Society, Conn. (2-6)

*52. Abby Bishop. **Sampler,** worked at Miss Mary Balch's school. Silk and wool on linen, 16 3/4″ x 19″ (42.6 x 48.3 cm). Providence, Rhode Island, signed and dated "1796." Museum of Fine Arts, Boston. Gift of Mrs. Samuel Cabot.

*53. Anonymous. **SACRED to the Memory of WASHINGTON.** Silk and watercolor on silk, 23″ (58.4 cm) in diameter. America, c. 1800-1815. Collection of Mr. and Mrs. Gregg Ring. (5)

*54. Anonymous. **Mourning picture.** Silk and watercolor on silk, 25 3/8″ (64.5 cm) in diameter, framed. Inscribed "In Memory of a Father/Shubael Abbe/Ob. April 16, 1804/ aged 59 years." Windham County, Connecticut, c. 1804-1810. Courtesy the Society for the Preservation of New England Antiquities, Boston. (1, 2, 3, 6)

*55. Eunice [Griswold] Pinney (1770-1849). **In Memory of Eunice Pinney.** Watercolor, ink, and pinpricks on paper, 16 1/2″ x 19 1/4″ (41.9 x 48.7 cm) oval. Connecticut, c. 1813. Museum of Fine Arts, Boston. M. and M. Karolik Collection. (1-3)

56. Eunice [Griswold] Pinney (1770-1849). **Memorial for Herself.** Watercolor and ink on paper, 16″ x 13 1/8″ (40.6 x 33.3 cm) framed. Inscribed "Sacred to the Memory of Mrs. Eunice Pinney who died — — — aged — — —." Connecticut, signed and dated "Drawn by Herself July 1813." New York State Historical Association, Cooperstown. (4-6)

*57. E. Smith. **Compleat Housewife: or, Accomplish'd Gentlewoman's Companion. Being A Collection of upwards of Six Hundred of the most approved Receipts in Cookery... To which is added A Collection of above Three Hundred Family Receipts of Medicines: viz. Drinks, Syrups, Salves, Ointments, and various other things of sovereign and approved Efficacy in most Distempers, Pains, Aches, Wounds, Sores, &c.** Printed book, 8″ x 5 1/4″ (20.3 x 13.4 cm). Fourteenth edition. London: Printed for R. Ware, S. Birt, T. Longman, C. Hitch, J. Hodges, J. and J. Rivington, J. Ward, W. Johnston, and M. Cooper, 1750. The Library Company of Philadelphia.

58. Lucy Emerson. **The NEW-ENGLAND COOKERY, or the ART of DRESSING ALL KINDS OF FLESH, FISH, AND VEGETABLES....** Printed book, 5 3/4″ x 3 1/2″ (14.6 x 8.8 cm). Montpelier [Vermont]: Printed for Josiah Parks, 1808. Collection of Esther Aresty.

59. Susannah Carter. **The Frugal Housewife, or Complete Woman Cook.** Printed book, 6 3/8″ x 3 7/8″ (16.2 x 9.8 cm). New York: Printed for Berry and Rogers, [1792]. The Library Company of Philadelphia.

60. Anonymous. **Pie marker.** Carved boxwood with copper wheel. 5 9/16″ x 1 21/32″ (14.1 x 4.2 cm). Inscribed "H. R." America, dated 1753. Philadelphia Museum of Art.

61. Anonymous. **Turner peel.** Wrought iron, 19″ x 6″ (48.3 x 15.2 cm). New England, 18th century. Pilgrim John Howland Society, Plymouth, Mass. (1)

62. Paul Revere II (1735-1818). **Skewer.** Silver, 9 1/4″ (23.5 cm). Mark "REVERE" in rectangle. Boston, 1796. Museum of Fine Arts, Boston. Gift of Pauline Revere Thayer.

63. Anonymous. **Larding pin.** Silver, 5 1/2″ (13.9 cm). America, c. 1790. Museum of Fine Arts, Boston. M. and M. Karolik Collection. (1)

64. Philip Miller. **The Gardners Dictionary.** Printed book, 8 1/16″ x 4 3/4″ x 1 9/16″ (20.5 x 13.4 x 4 cm). London: Sold by John and James Rivington, 1754. Library of the Massachusetts Horticultural Society, Boston.

65. Bernard M'Mahon (c. 1775-1816). **The AMERICAN GARDENER'S CALENDAR: Adapted to the Climates and Seasons of the UNITED STATES.** Printed book, 8 3/4″ x 5 1/2″ x 2 1/4″ (22.2 x 13.9 x 5.7 cm). Philadelphia: Printed by B. Graves, 1806. Library of the New York Botanical Garden, Bronx, N.Y.

66. Anonymous. **Candle box.** Painted pine, 5 5/8″ x 12″ x 6 1/4″ (14.2 x 50.5 x 15.9 cm). Pennsylvania, c. 1800. Lent by the Metropolitan Museum of Art. Gift of Mrs. Robert W. de Forest, 1933.

*67. Anonymous. **Basket.** Cane, 4 3/4″ x 7 1/2″ x 6″ (12 x 19.1 x 15.2 cm). Cherokee, c. 1730-1780. Courtesy the Peabody Museum of Archaeology and Ethnology, Cambridge, Mass.

68. Anonymous. **Woman's Calico Blouse.** Decorated with 3 trade silver brooches, 26″ x 55″ (66 x 124.7 cm). Oneida tribe, New York, c. 1860-1870. Museum of the American Indian, New York.

*69. Anonymous. **Hunting pouch.** Cloth, beads, 9″ x 7 3/4″ (22.9 x 19.6 cm) without fringe. Cherokee, late 18th or early 19th century. Courtesy the Peabody Museum of Archaeology and Ethnology, Cambridge, Mass.

70. Anonymous. **Black pouch Thunderbird.** Leather, quillwork, 8 1/2″ x 6″ (21.6 x 15.2 cm) without strap. Iroquois, c. 1750. Courtesy the Peabody Museum of Archaeology and Ethnology, Cambridge, Mass.

71. Anonymous. **Robe.** Deerskin with quillwork, 48″ x 58″ (121.9 x 147.3 cm). Iroquois, late 18th century. Courtesy the Peabody Museum of Archaeology and Ethnology, Cambridge, Mass.

*72. Anonymous. **Short gown.** Printed cotton. Pennsylvania, c. 1790-1810. Chester County Historical Society, West Chester, Pa.

*73. **Open robe.** Block-printed linen. Pennsylvania, c. 1740-1790. Chester County Historical Society, West Chester, Pa.

74. Anonymous. **Quilted petticoat.** Linen, cotton. America, c. 1790. Textile Resource and Research Center, Valentine Museum, Richmond, Va.

*75. Anonymous. **Bed rugg.** Wool with embroidered wool knots, seamed, 84 1/2″ x 66″ (203.2 x 167.6 cm). Probably Loudoun or Clarke County, Virginia, c. 1770-1800. Association for the Preservation of Virginia Antiquities, Richmond. Gift of Miriam K. Richards.

76. Anonymous. **Bed curtain** (one of a pair). Crewels on linen, 79 1/4″ x 31 1/2″ (201.3 x 80 cm). Connecticut, c. 1740-1780. A North Carolina collection.

*77. Esther Wheat (1774-1847). **Quilt.** Glazed wool, wool filling and lining (later wool lining added), 91″ x 93″ (231.1 x 236.2 cm). Conway, Massachusetts, c. 1790. Smithsonian Institution, Washington, D.C.

78. Anonymous. **Rug.** Wool on wool, 27″ x 56″ 68.6 x 142.2 cm). Made for E. D. Gifford, New England (?), c. 1800-1835. The New-York Historical Society. (6)

*79. Anonymous. **Pieced quilt.** Homespun linen and wool, wool padding, 76 1/2″ x 62 1/2″ (194.3 x 158.8 cm). America, c. 1790-1820. Museum of Early Southern Decorative Arts, Winston-Salem, N.C.

80. Mary Walker Stith. **Coverlet.** Cotton open work with cotton embroidery on linen, 96″ x 86″. (243.8 x 218.4 cm). Hardin County, Kentucky, c. 1815-1820. Lent by the Metropolitan Museum of Art. Fletcher Fund, 1939. (1-3)

*81. Anonymous. **Blanket.** Wool embroidered with crewels, 96″ x 80″ (243.9 x 203.2 cm). America, c. 1770. Greenfield Village and Henry Ford Museum, Dearborn, Mich.

*82. Cephas Thompson [attrib.] (1775-1856). **Elizabeth Wyche** (?) (1771-1819). Oil on canvas, 31 1/2″ x 21 1/2″ (80 x 54.7 cm). Virginia, c. 1800-1810. Collection of Mrs. John Van B. Metts.

*83. Anonymous. **Work table.** Mahogany and bird's-eye maple with painted decoration; secondary wood, pine, 28 1/4″ x 20 1/2″ x 15 1/4″ (71.8 x 52.1 x 38.8 cm). Portland, Maine (?), c. 1810. Museum of Fine Arts, Boston.

84. Anonymous. **Tape loom.** Wood inlaid with pewter, 23 1/2″ x 7 3/4″ x 1/4″ (59.6 x 19.6 x .6 cm). Inscribed "L. W." Rhode Island, late 18th century. The New-York Historical Society.

85. Anonymous. **Needlecase with needles.** Maple, steel, brass, 3 1/4″ x 11/16″ (8.2 x 1.8 cm). America, 18th century. The Colonial Williamsburg Foundation, Williamsburg, Va.

86. Anonymous. **Spinularium** with chain (to hold pincushion). Silver, 2″ (5.1 cm) in diameter. Engraved "Rachel * Lord * Her * Spinularium * October 20th 1765." Connecticut (?), c. 1760-1765. The Connecticut Historical Society, Hartford.

*87. Anonymous. **Chatelaine** with sewing tools. Silver, steel; pincushion worked in silk on canvas, 26″ (66 cm); pincushion, 2 1/4″ (10.8 cm) in diameter; scissors, 4 1/2″ (11.4 cm). Pennsylvania, 1799. Chester County Historical Society, West Chester, Pa.

88. Anonymous. **Pole screen.** Mahogany with pine, embroidered panel of wool and silk yarns and paint on linen worked by a member of the Revere family, 64 1/2″ x 22 1/2″ (163.8 x 57.2 cm); screen, 27 3/4″ (70.5 cm). Boston, c. 1760-1790. Museum of Fine Arts, Boston. Request of Mrs. Pauline Revere Thayer. (1)

89. "B. W." **Belt.** Leather, brass, worked in wools on canvas, 5″ x 41 1/8″ (12.7 x 104.5 cm). Baltimore (?). Inscribed and dated "James Cox his Belt / Worked by B W 1766." Collection of the Maryland Historical Society, Baltimore.

*90. Anonymous. **Pocketbook.** Wool on canvas, silk, 4 3/8″ x 6 1/2″ (11.1 x 16.6 cm). Pennsylvania, dated under flap "1776." Chester County Historical Society, West Chester, Pa.

*91. Anonymous. **Pockets.** Wool on canvas, 13″ x 10″ (31 x 25.4 cm). Pennsylvania, c. 1740-1790. Chester County Historical Society, West Chester, Pa.

92. Anonymous. **Seat cushion.** Crewels on linen, 19″ x 21 1/8″ (48.4 x 53.7 cm). New England, c. 1750. Courtesy Society for the Preservation of New England Antiquities, Boston. (1, 2, 3, 6)

*93. John Greenwood (1727-1792). **Jersey Nanny** (Ann Arnold). Mezzotint, 11″ x 9″ (27.9 x 22.9 cm). Signed, lower left, "Greenwood ad. vivum prinxt et fecit." Boston: Printed by J. Turner [1748].From the original in the Museum of·Fine Arts, Boston. Gift of Henry L. Shattuck.

*94. Eliza (Lucas) Pinckney (1722?-1793). Letter to "My dear Child," Autograph manuscript, 10 1/4″ x 8″ (25.5 x 20.3 cm). South Carolina, September 10, 1785. From the original at the Charleston Library Society, S.C.

95. Thomas Jefferys after William de Brahm, *et al.* **A Map of South Carolina and a Part of Georgia.** Hand-colored engraving, 28 27/32″ x 49 2/3″ (72 x 126.5 cm). London: October 20, 1757. The Charleston Museum Collection, S.C.

96. Anonymous. **For Sale, At Miss Goldwait's Shop.** Broadside completed in manuscript. 13 3/8″ x 8 1/4″ (34 x 21 cm), Boston, c. 1800. Trustees of the Boston Public Library.

*97. Anonymous. **Priscilla Abbot, At her Shop...** Receipt, printed and completed in manuscript, 7 9/32″ x 4 17/32″ (18.5 x 11.5 cm). Salem, Massachusetts, April 19, 1794. Courtesy Massachusetts Historical Society, Boston. (1)

*98. **The Maryland, Delaware, Pennsylvania, Virginia, and North-Carolina Almanack, and Ephemeris....** Printed almanac, 6 3/4″ x 4 1/8″ (17.2 x 10.5 cm). Baltimore: Printed and Sold...by M. K. Goddard, 1781. Library of the Maryland Historical Society, Baltimore.

*99. Anonymous. **Life, Last Words and Dying Confession of RACHEL WALL....** Broadside, 17 1/2″ x 13 9/16″ (44.5 x 34.5 cm) Boston, 1789. Courtesy Massachusetts Historical Society, Boston. (1)

100. Sarah Savage. **The Factory Girl.** Printed book, 5 3/4″ x 3 1/4″ (14.6 x 8.3 cm). Boston: Printed by Monroe, Francis, and Parker, 1814. American Antiquarian Society, Worcester, Mass. (1)

101. Eliza Anderson [Godefroy] (trans.). **MILITARY REFLECTIONS, on Four Modes of Defense, for the United States....** Printed book, 8 3/8″ x 5″ (21.3 x 12.7 cm). Baltimore: Printed by Joseph Robinson, 1807. Library of the Maryland Historical Society, Baltimore.

102. Anonymous. **Mitten.** Fur, deerskin, 8 1/2″ x 5 1/2″ (21.5 x 13.9 cm). Iroquois, early 19th century. Courtesy the Peabody Museum of Archaeology and Ethnology, Cambridge, Mass.

*103. Anonymous. **ELIZABETH CANNING, Drawn from the Life, as she stood at the Bar to Receive her Sentence, in the Session's House, in the Old-Bailey.** Hand-colored etching, 16″ x 10 5/16″ (40.6 x 26.1 cm) overall. London, 1754. The Historical Society of Pennsylvania, Philadelphia.

*104. Anonymous. **The Fortunate Transport, Rob. Thief, or the Lady of ye Gold Watch Poly Haycock.** Engraving, 11 1/4″ x 15 3/4″ (28.6 x 40 cm). England, c. 1760-1780. The Colonial Williamsburg Foundation, Williamsburg, Va.

105. **The Almshouse and House of Employment, City of Philadelphia, and Margaret Risk, Middletown Township, Bucks County. Indenture of Catharine Potts, aged thirteen years, an. Apprentice to serve Margaret Risk for five years.** Printed and completed in manuscript, 13″ x 8″ (33 x 20.3 cm). Bucks County, Pennsylvania, December 12, 1808. The Historical Society of Pennsylvania, Philadelphia.

*106. Anonymous. **TO BE SOLD,...A CARGO OF NINETY-FOUR PRIME, HEALTHY NEGROES.** Broadside, 12 1/2″ x 7 3/4″ (31.8 x 19.7 cm). Charlestown [S.C.], July 24th, 1769. American Antiquarian Society, Worcester, Mass. (1)

*107. Robert Matthew Sully [attrib.] (1803-1855). **Mammy Sally Brown.** Oil on canvas, 31 3/32″ x 26 1/16″ (81.2 x 66.2 cm). Virginia, c. 1842. Courtesy Massachusetts Historical Society, Boston. (1)

*108. Anonymous. **The Mirror of Misery; or, Tyranny Exposed.** Printed Book, 6 1/4″ x 4″ (15.9 x 10.1 cm). New York: Printed and Sold by Samuel Wood, 1811. The Historical Society of Pennsylvania, Philadelphia.

*109. Anonymous. **Bilhah Abigail Levy Franks** (Mrs. Jacob, 1696-1756). Oil on canvas, 44″ x 35″ (111.7 x 88.9 cm). New York c. 1740. The American Jewish Historical Society, Waltham, Mass.

*110. Thomas Sully [attrib.] (1783-1872). **Rebecca Gratz** (1781-1869). Oil on canvas, 20″ x 17″ (51 x 43.2 cm). Philadelphia, begun in 1830. Delaware Art Museum, Wilmington.

111. Anonymous. **Hanukkah lamp.** Tin, iron, 11″ (27.9 cm). Ipswich (?), Massachusetts, c. 1790-1820. Collection of Mr. and Mrs. Samuel Schwartz.

*112. Anonymous. **Marie Elizabeth Blum** (1743-1817). Oil on poplar, 9 3/8″ x 6 3/4″ (23.8 x 17.2 cm). Salem, North Carolina, or Pennsylvania, c. 1802-1817. Old Salem, Inc. Winston-Salem, N.C.

113. Anonymous. **Moravian haube.** Linen, silk ribbons, 8″ x 8″ (20.3 x 20.3 cm). North Carolina (?), 19th century. Old Salem, Inc., Winston-Salem, N.C.

*114. I. Rod Holzhald. **"Marriage de 12 Couples de Colonists"** (Marriage of 12 Colonial [Moravian] Couples). Top section of a double engraving, 22″ x 15 1/4″ (58.9 x 38.8 cm) overall, framed. From **Kurze, Zururlässige, Nachrecht Von der, unter dem Namen der Böhmisch- Mährischer Brüder bekannten, Kirsche UNITAS FRATRUM**...[Germany, 1757] or **Brèvre et Fidele Exposition de L'origine, de la Doctune...de Frères de Bohème**...[France, 1758] Old Salem, Inc. Winston-Salem, N.C.

*115. Anonymous. **Quaker Meeting.** Oil on canvas. 25″ x 30″ (63.5 x 76.2 cm). America, c. 1790. Museum of Fine Arts, Boston. M. and M. Karolik Collection.

116. Anonymous. **Quaker hat.** White beaver, 18″ (45.6 cm) in diameter. Pennsylvania, c. 1790-1810. Chester County Historical Society, West Chester, Pa.

*117. S[ophia] Hume (1702-1774). **An EXHOR-TATION TO THE INHABITANTS of the Province Of SOUTH-CAROLINA, to bring their Deeds To the Light of Christ, in their own Consciences.** Printed book, 7 1/2″ x 4″ (9.1 x 10.2 cm). Philadelphia: Printed by B[enjamin] Franklin and D.[avid] Hall, 1748. Boston Athenaeum.

118. James A. Weld after S. C. Cleveland. **Jemima Wilkinson (1752-1819).** Photograph of the lost original engraving, 6 1/2″ x 4 1/2″ (16.5 x 11.4 cm). New York, 1872. The Oliver House Museum. Yates County Genealogical and Historical Society, Inc., Penn Yan, N.Y.

*119. D. W. Kellogg. **SHAKERS. their mode of Worship.** Lithograph, 8″ x 10″ (20.3 x 25.4 cm). Hartford, Connecticut, c. 1835. From the original at the Shaker Museum, Old Chatham, N.Y.

120. Minerva Brewster Langworthy. **Shaker sampler.** Wool on linen, 5 1/4″ x 7 1/8″ (13.4 x 18.1 cm) framed. Hancock, Massachusetts, or Mount Lebanon, New York, signed and dated "MINERVA BREWSTER/LANG-WORTHY BORN/DECEMBER THE TWE/NTY FIFTH EIGHTEEN/HUNDRED SEVEN HER/EXAMPLE MARKED IN/THE YEAR EIGHTEEN/HUNDRED NINETEEN. The Shaker Museum, Old Chatham, N.Y.

121. Anonymous. **Oval Shaker box.** Maple (sides) and pine (top and bottom), copper, 2 1/4″ x 5 3/4″ x 3 7/8″ (5.7 x 14.6 x 9.8 cm). Alfred, Maine, c. 1870. The Shaker Museum, Old Chatham, N.Y.

122. Anonymous. **Shaker rocking chair.** Pine, bird's-eye maple, 45 1/2″ x 21 1/2″ x 23 1/2″ (115.6 x 54.6 x 59.6 cm). Owned by Sister Molly Smith (1780-1867) and Elderess Emma Neale (1846-1943). Mount Lebanon, New York, c. 1775-1840. The Philadelphia Museum of Art.

*123. Harriet Sewall. **The Orphans.** Watercolor and ink on paper, 14 3/4″ x 21 5/16″ (37.5 x 54.1 cm). New England (?) signed, dated and inscribed "1808 $10 Paid." Museum of Fine Arts, Boston. M. and M. Karolik Collection. (1-3)

124. Mrs. J. Akin (active c. 1803). **Membership Certificate in the Female Charitable Asylum for the Protection of Indigent Orphans.** Engraving, 15 3/4″ x 9 15/16″ (40 x 25.2 cm). Newbury-port, Massachusetts, 1803. Worcester Art Museum, Mass. (4-6)

125. Anonymous. **Scholastic medals.** Silver, 1 1/2″ x 1″ (3.8 x 2.5 cm) each. Awarded by the Female Orphan Asylum of Petersburg for industry, scholarship, and general merit. Petersburg (?), Virginia, 1814. The Virginia Historical Society, Richmond.

*126. Leonard Woods, D.D. **A SERMON, preached at Haverhill, (Mass.) in Remembrance of Mrs. HARRIET NEWELL, wife of the REV. SAMUEL NEWELL, missionary to India…to which are added MEMOIRS OF HER LIFE.** Printed book, 6″ x 3 1/2″ (15.2 x 8.9 cm). Fourth edition. Boston: Printed for Samuel T. Armstrong, Oct[ober], 1814. Boston Athenaeum.

*127. Anonymous. **The Takeing of Miss Mud I'land.** Engraving, 8 15/16″ x 7 1/4″ (22.7 x 18.4 cm). London, c. December 1777. Trustees of the British Museum, London.

128. **A Providence Gazette Extraordinary.** Newspaper, 15″ x 12 1/4″ (38.1 x 34.1 cm). Providence, Rhode Island: Printed by S. & W. Goddard, April 24, 1765. From the original in the Library of the Rhode Island Historical Society, Providence.

*129. **In CONGRESS, July 4, 1776 the unanimous DECLARATION of the Thirteen United States of AMERICA.** Broadside, 26″ x 21″ (66 x 53.3 cm), matted. Baltimore: Printed by Mary Katharine Goddard, 1777. From the original in the Library of Congress, Washington, D.C.

*130. Fidelia [Hannah Griffitts, 1727-1817]. **Beware of the Ides of March….** Autograph manuscript poem, 8 1/2″ x 6 1/2″ (21.6 x 16.5 cm). [Philadelphia] February 28, 1775. The Historical Society of Pennsylvania, Philadelphia.

131. [Hannah Griffitts, 1727-1817] **"Inscription, on a Curious Chamberstove, in ye form of an urn. Contributed in such a manner, as To Make ye flame discend, instead of rising; invented by ye Celebrated B.[enjamin] F.[ranklin]."** Autograph manuscript poem, copy, 8 9/32″ x 6 9/16″ 21 x 16.7 cm). [Philadelphia] November, 1776. The Historical Society of Pennsylvania, Philadelphia.

*132. Anonymous. **The Sentiments of an American Woman.** Broadside, 13 5/8″ x 8 1/2″ (34.6 x 21.5 cm), [Philadelphia, 10 June 1780]. The Historical Society of Pennsylvania, Philadelphia.

*133. Anonymous. **A Society of Patriotic Ladies, at Edenton in North Carolina.** Mezzotint and engraving, 13 1/8″ x 10″ (33.3 x 25.4 cm). London: Printed for R. Sayer and J. Bennett, March 25, 1775. Courtesy the Boston Public Library.

*134. Anonymous. **An Address to New-England: written by A Daughter of Liberty.** Broadside, 14 3/4″ x 8 7/8″ (37.5 x 22.5 cm). [Boston, 1774.] The Historical Society of Pennsylvania, Philadelphia.

*135. John Hoppner R.A. (1758-1810). **Sarah Franklin Bache (1743-1808).** Oil on canvas, 30 1/8″ x 24 7/8″ (76.5 x 37.8 cm). London, 1797. Lent by the Metropolitan Museum of Art. Wolfe Fund, 1901.

136. Anonymous. **Shirt** (worn by Colonel William Ledyard when he was killed by the British at the Battle of Ford Griswold, September 6, 1781). Linen. Connecticut, c. 1780-1781. The Connecticut Historical Society, Hartford.

*137. Anonymous. **A New Touch on the Times. Well adapted to the distressing Situation of every Sea-port Town. By a Daughter of Liberty, living in Marblehead.** Broadside, 13″ x 8 1/4″ (33 x 20.9 cm.) [Massachusetts, 1779]. The New-York Historical Society. (6)

138. Christiana Gatter. **Testimony of Rape by British Soldiers.** Autograph manuscript copy, 12 5/8″ x 7 3/16″ (32 x 18.3 cm). Deposition taken in New Haven, Connecticut, July 26th, 1779. Records of the United States Senate, National Archives, Washington, D.C.

139. **Camp Follower's clothing.** A modern reconstruction of clothing worn by camp followers in the American Revolution, based on descriptions found in contemporary writings.

140. Anonymous. **Molly Pitcher.** Carved wood, 26 1/2″ (67.3 cm) without base. America, 19th century. Museum of Fine Arts, Boston. M. and M. Karolik Collection.

*141. Joseph Stone. **Deborah Sampson** (Gannett, 1761-1827). Oil on paper, 17 1/2″ x 13 1/2″ (44.5 x 34.3 cm) framed. Signed and dated "Drawn by Joseph Stone Framingham, [Massachusetts] 1797." The Rhode Island Historical Society, Providence.

142. Deborah (Sampson) Gannett (1761-1827). **Petition to the United States for a Military Pension for Active Service in the American Revolution.** Autograph manuscript, 11 5/8″ x 7 1/4″ (29.5 x 18.4 cm). Massachusetts, September 14, 1818. National Archives, Washington, D.C. (6)

*143. James Calhoun, Jr. (Deputy Commissary of Fort McHenry). **Receipt to Mary Pickersgill for making flags.** Autograph manuscript, 5″ x 7″ (12.7 x 17.8 cm). Baltimore, August 19, 1813. From the original at the Star Spangled Banner Flag House Association, Inc., Baltimore.

*144. John Singleton Copley (1738-1815). **Mercy Otis Warren** (Mrs. James, 1728-1814). Oil on canvas, 51 1/4″ x 41″ (130.2 x 104.1 cm). Boston, c. 1763. Museum of Fine Arts, Boston. Bequest of Winslow Warren. (2-6)

*145. Mercy Otis Warren (1728-1814). **History of the Rise, Progress, and Termination of the American Revolution...**, Vol. I. 8 1/2″ x 5 1/2″ x 1/2″ (21.5 x 13.9 x 1.3 cm). Boston: Printed by Manning and Loring, 1805. Copyright ☉ The Pilgrim Society, Plymouth, Mass.

*146. Anonymous. **Card table.** Mahogany with pine and maple, wool embroidered top worked by Mercy Otis Warren, 27 1/4″ x 41 1/8″ x 38 1/2″ (69.2 x 53.7 x 97.8 cm) open. Boston (table) and Plymouth, c. 1750-1770. Copyright☉ The Pilgrim Society, Plymouth, Mass.

147. Anonymous. **Fish.** Mother-of-pearl. 2 1/2″ (6.4 cm) average. England (?), 18th century. Copyright ☉The Pilgrim Society, Plymouth, Mass.

148. Mercy Otis Warren (?) (1728-1814). **Pincushion.** Silk on silk, 6 3/4″ x 3″ (17.2 x 7.6 cm). Massachusetts (?), c. 1750-1780. Courtesy the Massachusetts Historical Society, Boston. (1)

*149. Anonymous. **Handkerchief pin,** worn by Abigail Adams. Gold, hair, pearls, glass, 3/8″ x 1 1/8″ x 1 1/4″ (.9 x 2.9 x .6 cm). Initials "MW" (Mercy Otis Warren) in gold script under glass. Massachusetts, 1812. Courtesy the Massachusetts Historical Society, Boston. (1)

*150. Anonymous. **Shoe,** owned by Mercy Otis Warren. Silk brocade, silver, leather, 9 1/2″ x 3″ (24.1 x 7.6 cm). England (?), c. 1750-1780. (c) The Plymouth Antiquarian Society, Plymouth, Mass.

*151. John Vanderlyn [attrib.] (1775-1852). **Theodosia Burr** (Mrs. Joseph Alston, 1783-1813). Oil on canvas (unfinished), 26 3/16″ x 22″ (66.5 x 55.9 cm). New York, c. 1815-1820. The New-York Historical Society.

*152. Chester Harding (1792-1866). **Hannah Adams** (1755-1831). Oil on canvas, 36″ x 27″ (91.4 x 68.6 cm). Boston (?), c. 1827. Boston Athenaeum.

153. Hannah Adams (1755-1831). **The History of the Jews, from the Destruction of Jerusalem to the Present Time.** Printed book, 8 1/2″ x 4 1/2″ x 1 1/2″ (21.6 x 11.4 x 3.8 cm). London: Printed by A. MacIntosh, 1818. Boston Athenaeum.

154. Hannah Adams (1755-1831). **AN ALPHABETICAL COMPENDIUM OF THE VARIOUS SECTS which have Appeared in the World from the beginning of the Christian Era To the present Day...** Printed book, 8″ x 5″ x 1 1/2″ (20.3 x 12.7 x 3.8 cm). Printed by B. Edes & Sons, 1784. Boston Athenaeum.

155. Jane Colden (Farquhar, 1724-1766). **Botanic Manuscript.** 12″ x 7″ (30.5 x 17.8 cm). New York, c. 1750-1757. Trustees of the British Museum, London, England.

*156. Linden Hall Seminary for Young Ladies, Lancaster County [Pennsylvania]. **Terms and Conditions of the Boarding School for Female Education in Litiz...January 6, 1809.** 9 1/4″ x 6 7/8″ (23.5 x 17.5 cm). [Lancaster, 1808 (?)] The Historical Society of Pennsylvania, Philadelphia.

157. Edward Moore. **FABLES for the LADIES.** Printed book, 5 1/8″ x 6 3/16″ (113 x 15.7 cm) open. Inscribed on page facing title page "Be it Known that this/Book was adjudged and/publickly presented by the/Visitors of Mr John Poor's/Academy on the third day/of December 1788 to Miss/Peggy McCullough of the/third Class as a Premium/for her superior excellence in/Reading—/By order of the Visitors/John Andrews Presidt./Test. Benjn Say Sec'ry." Philadelphia: Printed for Thomas Dobson, 1787. The Historical Society of Pennsylvania, Philadelphia.

158. Patty Coggeshall. **Sampler.** Silk on linen, 19 1/2″ x 16 5/8″ (49.5 x 42.2 cm). Signed and inscribed "Patty Coggeshall Born/Feb 15th, 1786 Bristol New E." Bristol, Rhode Island, 1795. Lent by the Metropolitan Museum of Art. Rogers Fund, 1901.

*159. Lydia Church. **Sampler,** worked at Mrs. Mansfield's school. Silk, sequins, and metallic threads on linen, 18 3/4″ x 20 3/4″ (47.8 x 53 cm). Inscribed "New Haven Connecticut• July 19 1791 Mrs Mansfield Sc/LYDIA CHURCH aged 13 1791." The Connecticut Historical Society, Hartford.

*160. Nabby Martin. **Sampler,** worked at Miss Balch's school. Silk on canvas, 15″ x 10 1/4″ (38.1 x 26 cm). Providence, Rhode Island, signed and dated "1786." Museum of Art, Rhode Island School of Design, Providence.

161. Amy Randall. **Sampler** (unfinished), worked at Miss Mary Balch's school. Silk on linen, 20 1/4″ x 19 1/2″ (51.4 x 49.5 cm). Providence, Rhode Island, signed and dated "1793." The Rhode Island Historical Society, Providence.

162. Anonymous. **Sampler frame.** Curly maple with silver inlay, 19″ x 11 1/4″ (48.3 x 28.6 cm). Silver inset plate inscribed "J. McILvain." Pennsylvania, late 18th century. The New-York Historical Society.

*163. Anonymous. **Terrestrial globe** worked at the Westtown School. Silk threads on silk, ink, 6 1/2″ (16.5 cm) in diameter. Chester County, Pennsylvania, c. 1810-1820. Chester County Historical Society, West Chester, Pa.

*164. "I.G." **Sampler.** Silk and linen on linen, 14″ x 9″ (35.6 x 22.9 cm) framed. Chester County (?), Pennsylvania, inscribed and dated "IG 1790." Chester County Historical Society, West Chester, Pa.

*165. Persis Crane. **Wisdom Leading Youth to Education.** Silk threads on silk, 15 1/2″ x 12 1/4″ (39.4 x 31.1 cm). Worked at Mrs. and Miss Beach's school. Dorchester, Massachusetts, 1812. Mr. and Mrs. Bertram K. Little.

166. Mary Beale (grandmother of Ann Marsh). **Sampler.** Silk on linen, 18 1/4″ x 8 1/4″ (46.4 x 20.9 cm) framed. England, signed and dated 1654. Collection of George Norman Highley.

167. Ann Marsh (1717-1797). **Sampler.** Silk on linen, 17″ x 13 1/4″ (43.2 x 33.7 cm) framed. Philadelphia (?), signed and dated, "Ann Marsh her Work in the 10 YEAR OF HER AGE 1727." Collection of George Norman Highley.

*168. Ann Marsh [attrib.] (1717-1797). **Needlework picture.** Silk on satin, silk border, 17 1/2″ x 10 1/4″ (44.5 x 26 cm). Pennsylvania (?), c. 1727-1760. Collection of Mrs. Lynmar Brock.

*169. Ann Marsh [attrib.] (1717-1797). **Seat cushion.** Silk and wool on canvas, 18 1/2″ x 21 3/4″ (47 x 55.3 cm). Pennsylvania, c. 1740-1790. Chester County Historical Society, West Chester, Pa.

*170. Ann Marsh [attrib.] (1717-1797). **Quilted petticoat.** Silk. Pennsylvania, c. 1740-1790. Chester County Historical Society, West Chester, Pa.

*171. Miss Prudence Perkins. **River—Townscape with Figures.** Transparent and opaque watercolor, colored inks on paper, 18 1/2″ x 22 3/4″ (46.9 x 57.7 cm). Providence (?), Rhode Island, c. 1810. Collection of Peter H. Tillou.

*172. John Durand [attrib.] (active 1766-1782). **Mrs. Lewis Burwell** (Lucy Randolph). Oil on canvas, 37″ x 29″ (94 x 73.7 cm). Virginia, c. 1770. Virginia Historical Society, Richmond.

*173. Gibson. **Playing cards.** Paper, 3 3/4″ x 2 1/2″ (9.5 x 6.4 cm). England, 1789-1804. The Colonial Williamsburg Foundation, Williamsburg, Va.

174. [John le Jeune] Faber (1684-1756) after Ph[ilippe] Mercier (1689-1760). **Music has Charms to sooth a Savage Breast.** Mezzotint, 14 1/8″ x 17 1/4″ (35.9 x 43.8 cm). London, March 25, 1774. The Library Company of Philadelphia.

175. J. Gillray. **Farmer Giles & His Wife Shewing (sic) off their daughter Betty to their neighbours on her return from school.** Hand-colored etching, 17″ x 23″ (43.2 x 58.4 cm). London: Published by H. Humphrey, January 1, 1809. Collection of James M. Goode.

*176. Jane Norton (?). **Chemise.** Linen, 40 3/4″ x 20 5/8″ (103.5 x 52.4 cm). Initials "IN" in cross-stitch at neck. Hingham (?) Massachusetts, c. 1800-1810. Courtesy Society for the Preservation of New England Antiquities, Boston.

177. Anonymous. **Open robe, with matching petticoat** (reproduction stomacher). Ribbed silk brocade, silk fringe. Descended in the family of Henry Middleton of South Carolina. French, (?) c. 1750-1760. The Charleston Museum Collection, S.C. 1740-1775.

*178. John Singleton Copley (1755-1815). **Mary MacIntosh and Elizabeth Royall.** Oil on canvas, 57 1/2″ x 48″ (146.1 x 121.9 cm). Boston, c. 1758. Museum of Fine Arts, Boston. Julia Knight Fox Fund. (2, 3, 4, 5)

179. Anonymous. **Dress.** Chintz, wood-block printed on a dark ground with floral sprays in madder colors. Connecticut, c. 1775. The Connecticut Historical Society, Hartford.

*180. Anonymous. **Lady's gown.** White muslin embroidered with cotton. New England, c. 1800-1810. Copyright © Plymouth Antiquarian Society, Mass.

181. Anonymous. **Shawl.** Muslin with cotton embroidery and drawnwork, 34″ x 109″ (86.4 x 276.9 cm). Worn by Julia Johnson Toler of Newark, N.J. America, c. 1810. The Newark Museum.

*182. Anonymous. **Lady's Cardinal.** Red wool, silk. Cazenovia, New York, late 18th century. Collection of Cora Ginsburg.

*183. Anonymous, after John Collet (1697-1764. **Tight Lacing, or Fashion before Ease.** Mezzotint, 16″ x 11 1/2″ (40.6 x 29.2 cm). London: Printed...& Sold by Bowles & Carver. c. 1770. American Antiquarian Society, Worcester, Mass. (1)

184. Anonymous, after John Collet (1697-1764). **Tight Lacing, or FASHION before EASE.** Hand-colored mezzotint, 18 1/4″ x 11 7/16″ (46.4 x 29.1 cm). London: Printed by Bowles & Carver, c. 1770. The Colonial Williamsburg Foundation, Williamsburg, Va. (2-6)

*185. Anonymous. **Stays.** Linen, bone. 15 1/2″ x 16″ (39.4 x 40.6 cm) closed. New England, c. 1770-1785. Copyright © Plymouth Antiquarian Society, Mass.

186. Anonymous. **Carved wooden busk.** 13 13/16″ x 2 7/16″ (35.1 x 6.2 cm). America, inscribed and dated "M M 1767·BE ⊞ GE." New York State Historical Association, Cooperstown.

*187. Anonymous. **Hey Day! Is this my Daughter Ann?** Hand-colored engraving, 22 3/8″ x 17 1/2″ (56.8 x 44.5 cm) framed. London: Printed for Carrington Bowles, June 14, 1774. Collection of Cora Ginsburg.

188. Anonymous. **Wig curler.** Iron, 10″ 25.4 cm). America, 18th century (?). Private collection.

*189. Anonymous. **Calash.** Silk, bone, 18 11/16″ x 20 9/32″ (47.5 x 51.5 cm). America, late 18th century. Philadelphia Museum of Art.

190. Anonymous. **Quilted bonnet.** Silk, 18 1/4″ x 13″ (46.4 x 33 cm). America, 19th century. Philadelphia Museum of Art.

191. Anonymous. **Hatbox.** Printed wallpaper on wood, 6″ x 12″ x 10 7/8″ (15.2 x 30.5 x 27.6 cm). America, c. 1800-1820. Courtesy Society for the Preservation of New England Antiquities, Boston.

192. Anonymous. **Lady's cap.** Spotted linen with mull fringe, 11″ x 10″ (27.9 x 25.4 cm). America, c. 1790-1810. Gift of Mr. Clifton Goff, Collection of the Brooklyn Museum, N.Y.

193. **Shoes worn by Eliza (Lucas) Pinckney** (1722?-1793). Satin with silver braid trim; silk lining, leather, 9 1/2″ x 3″ (23 x 7.6 cm). Label: "Made by / Thos H--e / Shoemaker No -/ Lombard St--/ London--," c. 1750-1775. The Charleston Museum Collection, S.C.

194. Jno Hose & Son. **Lady's shoes.** Silk brocade, leather, 9 1/2″ x 3″ (24.1 x 7.6 cm). London, c. 1750-1785. Courtesy Society for the Preservation of New England Antiquities, Boston.

195. Anonymous. **Lady's shoes.** Yellow and black kid, leather. 10″ x 3 3/4″ (25.4 x 9.5 cm). America, c. 1790-1810. Courtesy Society for the Preservation of New England Antiquities, Boston.

*196. Anonymous. **Pattens.** Leather, iron, replacement hide strings, 2 3/8″ x 8 1/2″ x 2 3/4″ (6 x 21.6 x 6.9 cm). Pennsylvania, c. 1760-1790. Chester County Historical Society, West Chester, Pa.

*197. Rufus Hathaway [attrib.] (1770-1822). **Sylvia Church Weston Sampson** (Mrs. Sylvanus, 1768-1836). Oil on canvas, 37 1/2″ x 25 1/4″ (95.3 x 64.2 cm). Duxbury, Massachusetts, 1793. Private collection.

198. Anonymous. **Perfume bottle.** Painted porcelain, brass, 3 7/8″ (9.8 cm). France or Germany, late 18th century. The New-York Historical Society.

199. Anonymous. **Perfume and cosmetics box.** Shagreen case containing gold funnel, four crystal perfume bottles with gold caps, mirror, and ivory-handled brush with gold cover, 1 7/8″ x 1 1/2″ (4.8 x 3.8 cm). France, c. 1750-1775. The Colonial Williamsburg Foundation, Williamsburg, Va.

*200. M. Buchoz. **The Toilet of Flora...with Receipts for Cosmetics of Every Kind, that can Smooth and brighten the Skin, give Force to Beauty, and Take off the Appearance of Old Age and Decay.** Printed book, 6 7/8″ x 4 3/8″ (17.5 x 11.1 cm). London: Printed for W. Nicholl, 1772. The Library Company of Philadelphia.

*201. Alexander S. Gordon (working 1795-1803). **Box, possibly a patch box.** Silver, 3/4 x 1 1/2″ x 1″ (1.91 x 3.9 x 2.5 cm). Marks: "GORDON" in serrated rectangle, initials "JTD" (?) in bright-cut engraving on lid. New York City, c. 1795-1803. Museum of the City of New York. Gift of Mrs. Charles E. Atwood.

202. Anonymous. **Chatelaine.** Gold and gold-filled, enamel, porcelain, 6 7/8″ x 2 3/4″ (17.5 x 6.9 cm). France (?), c. 1780-1790. Collection of Arthur Guy Kaplan.

*203. Elizabeth Shurtlef (?). **Pocketbook.** Wool on canvas, 3″ x 7″ (7.6 x 17.8 cm). Plymouth (?), Massachusetts, c. 1740-1790. (c) Plymouth Antiquarian Society, Plymouth, Mass.

204. Anonymous. **Reticule.** Satin with silk and silver threads, 10″ (25.4 cm). New Jersey (?), c. 1800-1810. Collection of the Newark Museum.

*205. E. M. Brevuort, **Beaded bag.** Beads on linen, silk lining, 8 1/4″ x 6 1/4″ (20.9 x 15.8 cm). America, c. 1810. Collection of Alvin and Davida Deutsch.

*206. Anonymous. **Fan.** Ivory, mother-of-pearl, white satin, brass, watercolor, 10 1/2″ x 17 1/2″ (26.6 x 44.5 cm) open. Chinese (?) for the American market, c. 1800-1825. The Litchfield Historical Society, Conn.

207. Anonymous. **Lady's mittens.** Silk worked with silk; linen facing, 13″ x 5 1/4″ (33 x 13.4 cm). England, c. 1750-1760. The Brooklyn Museum, N.Y.

208. Anonymous. **Lady's stockings.** Silk embroidered with silk, 20 3/4″ x 7″ (52.7 x 17.8 cm). Marked "B (?) FARRAN." America, c. 1750-1760. The Brooklyn Museum, N.Y.

209. Anonymous. **Apron.** Embroidered linen, 42″ x 48″ (106.7 x 121.9 cm). America, c. 1790-1800. Gift of Mrs. Tracy Voorhees, Collection of the Brooklyn Museum, N.Y.

*210. Patience Lovell Wright (1725-1786). **Lord Chatham** (William Pitt, the Elder). Clothed wax figure, life size. London, completed in 1779. From the original at Westminister Abbey.

211. Anonymous. **Mrs. Wright** (Patience Lovell Wright, 1725-1786). Engraving, 8 5/32″ x 5 1/16″ (20.7 x 12.8 cm). From the **London Magazine,** December 1, 1775. The Library of Congress, Washington, D.C.

212. M[atthew] Darly. **THE HEADS OF THE NATION IN A RIGHT SITUATION.** Engraving, 8 1/8″ x 12 13/16″ (20.6 x 32.5). London, May 1, 1780. The Lewis Walpole Library, Farmington, Conn.

213. Sophia Burpee [attrib.]. **Morning.** Watercolor and ink on paper, 10 7/8″ x 8 1/5″ (27.6 x 20.8 cm). New England, c. 1800-1810. The Abby Aldrich Rockefeller Folk Art Collection, Williamsburg, Va.

214. Rebecca Couch [attrib.] **Connecticut House.** Watercolor on paper, 13″ x 16 3/8″ (33 x 41.6 cm). Litchfield (?) or Redding (?), Connecticut, c. 1800-1825. The Abby Aldrich Rockefeller Folk Art Collection, Williamsburg, Va.

*215. Hetty Benbridge [attrib.] **John Poage.** Watercolor on ivory, gold, glass, 2 1/8″ x 1 9/16″ (5.4 x 3.9 cm). Charleston, South Carolina, c. 1773. Greenfield Village and Henry Ford Museum, Dearborn, Mich.

*216. Eunice [Griswold] Pinney (1770-1849). **Charlotte's Visit to the Vicar.** Watercolor and ink on paper, 13 1/2″ x 9 3/4″ (34.3 x 24.8 cm). Connecticut, signed and dated at bottom "Eunice Pinney's Drawing, 1810." Collection of Edgar William and Bernice Chrysler Garbisch.

217. Eunice [Griswold] Pinney [attrib.] (1770-1849). **The Courtship.** Watercolor on paper, 12 1/2″ x 9 1/2″ (31.8 x 24.1 cm). Connecticut, c. 1810. Collection of Edgar William and Bernice Chrysler Garbisch.

218. Eunice [Griswold] Pinney (1770-1849). **Children Playing.** Watercolor, ink, and pinpricks on paper, 5 3/8″ x 8″ (13.7 x 20.3 cm). Connecticut, signed and dated "Eunice Pinney's Drawing, 1813." Collection of Peter H. Tillou.

219. Eunice [Griswold] Pinney [attrib.] (1770-1849). **The Cotter's Saturday Night.** Watercolor and ink on paper, 12 1/8″ x 14 5/8″ (30.8 x 37.2 cm). Connecticut, c. 1815. National Gallery of Art, Washington, D.C. Gift of Edgar William and Bernice Chrysler Garbisch. (5, 6)

220. Eunice [Griswold] Pinney [attrib.] (1770-1849). **Landscape with Women.** Watercolor on paper, 13 1/8″ x 15 3/8″ (33.3 x 39.1 cm). Connecticut, c. 1810. Collection of Edgar William and Bernice Chrysler Garbisch.

221. Anne-Marguerite-Henriette-Rouille (de Marigny), Baroness Hyde de Neuville [attrib.], (1779?-1849). **Self-Portrait.** Pencil and watercolor on paper, 6 1/2″ x 5 5/8″ (16.5 x 14.3 cm). New York, c. 1807-1809. The New-York Historical Society. (6)

*222. Baroness Hyde de Neuville [attrib.] (1779?-1849). **Scrubwoman.** Watercolor and pen on paper, 7 1/2″ x 6 1/2″ (19.1 x 16.5 cm). Inscribed at bottom "Costume de Scrobeuse d'après Jene nièce de Martha Church." New York, c. 1807-1809. The New-York Historical Society.

*223. Baroness Hyde de Neuville [attrib.] (1779?-1849). **Indian War Dance.** Watercolor, ink, and pencil on paper, 7 5/8″ x 12″ (19.4 x 30.5 cm). Washington, D.C., inscribed and dated at bottom "Danse Militaire des Sauvages devant Le President J. Monroe 1821." Abby Aldrich Rockefeller Folk Art Collection, Williamsburg, Va.

*224. Mary Ann Willson [attrib.] (working c 1800-1825). **Nuestra Senora demonte Carmelo** (Our Lady of Mount Carmel). Pen and watercolor on paper, 12 1/8″ x 9 11/16″ (31.8 x 24.6 cm). Greene County, New York, c. 1800-1825. Museum of Fine Arts, Boston. M. & M. Karolik Collection. (1-3)

225. Mary Ann Willson [attrib.] (working 1800-1825). **Young Woman Pointing to Flight of Birds.** Watercolor on paper, 7 15/16″ x 6 1/2″ (20.2 x 16.5 cm). Greene County, New York, c. 1800-1825. Museum of Fine Arts, Boston. M. & M Karolik Collection. (1-3)

*226. Mary Ann Wilson [attrib.] (working 1800-1825).**The Leave Taking.** Pen and watercolor on paper, 13 11/16″ x 10 11/16″ (34.8 x 27.2 cm). Greene County, New York, c. 1800-1825. Museum of Fine Arts, Boston. M. & M. Karolik Collection. (4-6)

*227. Anna Maria von Phul [attrib.] (1786-1823). **Creole Woman and Boy.** Watercolor and pencil on paper, 9 7/8″ x 7 3/4″ (25.1 x 19.7 cm). St. Louis, Missouri, c. 1818. Missouri Historical Society, St. Louis.

228. Anna Maria von Phul [attrib.] (1786-1823. **Young Lady in a Garden.** Pencil and watercolor on paper, 8 3/4″ x 6 3/4″ (22.2 x 17.2 cm). St. Louis, Missouri, c. 1818. The Missouri Historical Society, St. Louis.

*229. Barbara Schultz [attrib.] **Schwenkfelder Birth Certificate of Lydia Kriebel,** born 1786. Watercolor and ink on paper, 16″ x 13″ (40.6 x 33 cm). Pennsylvania, dated "1806." Private Collection. (4-6)

229A. Susanna Hübner. **Schwenkfelder Religious Illuminations.** Double fractur (a & b). Watercolor and ink on paper, (a) 8 1/4″ x 13 1/4″ (21 x 33.6 cm) signed on reverse, Pennsylvania, c. 1810; (b) 7 7/8″ x 13 1/4″ (20 x 33.6 cm), Pennsylvania, dated August 28, 1808. The Schwenkfelder Library, Pennsburg, Pa. (1, 2, 3)

*230. Samuel F. B. Morse (?) (1791-1872). **Susanna Haswell Rowson** (?) (1762?-1824). Oil on canvas, 29 15/16″ x 25 9/16″ (76 x 64.9 cm) unframed. America, c. 1800-1825. Worcester Art Museum, Mass.

231. Mrs. Susanna [Haswell] Rowson (1762?-1824). **An Abridgement of Universal Geography.** Printed book, 7″ x 4 1/4″ (17.8 x 10.8 cm). Boston: Printed by David Carlisle, 1805. American Antiquarian Society, Worcester, Mass. (1)

232. Margaret Mitchell (b. Peterborough, N.H., 1784, d. 1867). **Quilted white bed coverlet.** Made while a student at Susanna Haswell Rowson's Academy. Cotton, linen, 75″ x 63″ (190.5 x 160 cm). Medford (?), Massachusetts, c. 1800. New Hampshire Historical Society, Concord. (4-6)

*233. Margaret Mitchell (b. Peterborough, New Hampshire, 1784, d. 1867). **Garden Lilly.** Done while a student at Mrs. Rowson's Academy. Watercolor and ink on paper, 8″ x 6 5/8″ (20.3 x 17.2 cm). Medford (?), Massachusetts, c. 1800. New Hampshire Historical Society, Concord.

234. Words by Susanna Haswell Rowson (1762?-1824). **National Song...4th of July.** Printed sheet music, 12″ x 20″ (30.5 x 50.8 cm) open. Boston: Published and sold by G. Graupner, 1818. American Antiquarian Society, Worcester, Mass. (1)

*235 Anonymous. **Mrs. David Douglass** (Mrs. Lewis Hallam, d. 1774). Watercolor on ivory, glass, gold, 2 1/2″ x 2″ (6.3 x 5 cm). America, c. 1756-1774. The Walter Hampden-Edwin Booth Theater Collection and Library, New York City.

*236. Southwark Theater. **For the Benefit of Miss Storer.** Playbill, 8 1/2″ x 5 3/4″ (21.6 x 14.6 cm). [Philadelphia: Printed by William Bradford, 1770.] Historical Society of Pennsylvania, Philadelphia.

237. The Old American Company. **MORE WAYS THAN ONE...to which will be added, ...DON JUAN...** Playbill, 17″ x 10 1/2″ (43.2 x 26.7 cm). New York City, March 12, 1793. Theater and Music Collection, Museum of the City of New York.

*238. R. Laurie, after R. Dighton. **Mrs. Wrighten** (Mrs. Pownall 1756?-1796). Mezzotint, 8 1/2″ x 6″ (21.6 x 15.2 cm). London: Published...by W. Richardson, March 1, 1780. The Metropolitan Museum of Art, Harris Brisbane Dick Fund, 1917.

*239. Gilbert Stuart (1755-1828). **Sarah Wentworth Apthorp Morton** (Mrs. Perez, 1759-1846). Oil on canvas, 29 1/4″ x 24″ (74.3 x 69.9 cm). Philadelphia, 1802. Museum of Fine Arts, Boston, Juliana Cheney Edwards Collection. Bequest of Hannah Marcy Edwards in memory of her mother.

240. Phillis Wheatley. **America.** Autograph manuscript poem, 11 3/4″ x 7 5/16″ (29.8 x 18.6 cm). Boston, c. 1770-1780. The Library Company of Philadelphia.

*241. Anonymous, after Gilbert Stuart (1755-1828) and Charles Willson Peale (1741-1827). **Martha (Dandridge Custis) Washington** (1731-1802). Oil on canvas, 30″ x 25 1/4″ (76.2 x 64.2 cm). America, 19th century. National Portrait Gallery, Smithsonian Institution, Washington, D.C.

*242. George Washington (1732-1799). **An account of Mrs. Washington's Expenses from Virginia to my Winter Quarters & back again during the Revolutionary War....** Autograph manuscript, 12 3/4″ x 8″ (32.4 x 20.3 cm). July 1, 1783. From the original at The Mount Vernon Ladies' Association, Mount Vernon, Va.

243. Anonymous. **Quarter panel of the coach owned by Martha Washington.** Painted copper, 17 1/16″ x 15″ (43.3 x 38.1 cm) framed. England, c. 1770, Smithsonian Institution, Washington, D.C.

244. Anonymous. **Invitation to the President's House** (Washington Administration). Engraving, 2 7/8″ x 4 14/16″ (7.3 x 12.5 cm). New York or Philadelphia, c. 1790-1797. Smithsonian Institution, Washington, D.C.

245. Martha Washington (1731-1802). **Letter to Frances Washington.** Autograph manuscript, 10″ x 7 7/8″ (25.4 x 20 cm). New York, October 22, 1789. The Historical Society of Pennsylvania, Philadelphia.

246. Anonymous. **Sewing box** owned by Martha Washington. Leather, wood, paper, containing thimble, scissors, fabrics, and embroidery, 3″ x 7 7/8″ (7.6 x 20 cm). America, late 18th century. The Chicago Historical Society, Ill.

*247. Martha Washington (1731-1802). **Seat cushion** (one of a set). Worsted and silk on canvas, 3″ x 18 3/4″ x 15 1/2″ (7.62 x 45.8 x 39.4 cm). Virginia, New York, or Philadelphia, c. 1766-1802. The Mount Vernon Ladies' Association, Mount Vernon. Va.

248. Anonymous. **Quilted cloak** owned by Martha Washington. Green silk. America, c. 1780-1800. Dumbarton House, Washington, D.C.

*249. Gilbert Stuart (1755-1828). **Mrs. John Adams** (Abigail Smith) 1744-1818). Oil on canvas, 29″ x 23 3/4″ (73.9 x 60.3 cm). Boston, 1815. National Gallery of Art, Washington, D.C. (2-6)

250. Anonymous. **Fan** owned by Abigail Adams (1744-1818). Silk, net, sequins, amber, 7 7/16″ x 13 11/16″ (18.8 x 34.8 cm). France (?), c. 1780-1800. Smithsonian Institution, Washington, D.C.

*251. Anonymous. **Dinner plate** (part of a set owned by John and Abigail Adams). Hand-painted blue and white porcelain, 1″ x 7 3/4″ (2.5 x 24.8 cm) in diameter. Marks and date letter of the Sèvres manufactory, France, 1784. Smithsonian Institution, Washington, D.C.

252. Anonymous. **Pocket-Book: A General Bill of Fare, for Every Month in the Year. Revised and Corrected, by an eminent City Cook, 1755.** 6 7/16″ x 4″ (16.4 x 10.2 cm) closed. England, c. 1775-1800. Owned by Abigail Adams (title page missing). Smithsonian Institution, Washington, D.C.

*253. Abigail [Smith] Adams. **Letter to John Adams.** Autograph manuscript, 12 13/21″ x 7 7/8″ (31.5 x 20 cm). Braintree, Massachusetts, March 31, 1776. Courtesy, Massachusetts Historical Society, Boston. (1)

*254. John Vanderlyn [attrib.] (1775-1852) after Gilbert Stuart (1755-1828). **Mrs. James Madison** (Dolley [Payne] Todd, 1768-1849). Oil on canvas, 35″ x 30″ (88.9 x 76.2 cm) framed. America, c. 1830-1850. Collection of the Greensboro Historical Museum, N.C.

*255. Anonymous. **Gown** worn by Dolley Madison (1768-1849). Red silk velvet with silver trim. America (?), c. 1800-1815. Collection of the Greensboro Historical Museum, N.C.

256. Anonymous. **Turban** worn by Dolley Madison (1768-1849). White silk with silk cord trim, 6″ x 9″ (15.2 x 22.3 cm). America or France, c. 1810-1840. Collection of the Greensboro Historical Museum, N.C.

257. Dolley Madison (1768-1849). **"Extract from a letter written (crossed-out) to my sister published in the sketch of my life written for the 'National Portrait Gallery'"** (Unsigned copy dated August 23, 1814 by her hand of the original letter of August 24, 1814) 9 7/8″ x 6 5/8″ (25.1 x 16.8 cm) uncased. Virginia or Washington, D.C., c. 1830-1849. From the original in the Department of Manuscripts, Library of Congress, Washington, D.C.

258. Anonymous. **The Lady's Magazine, and Repository of Entertaining Knowledge.** Printed magazine, 8 1/2″ x 5 3/16″ x 1″ (21.5 x 13.2 x 2.5 cm). Vol. I By a Literary Society. Philadelphia: Printed by W: Gibbons, 1792. The Library Company of Philadelphia.

259. Mary Wollstonecraft (1759-1797). **A Vindication of the Rights of Woman: with strictures on Political and Moral Subjects.** Printed book, 8 9/16″ x 5 5/16″ (27.7 x 13.5 cm). Boston: Printed by Peter Edes for Thomas and Andrews, 1792. The Library Company of Philadelphia.

*260. Susan Sedgwick. **Elizabeth Freeman (Mumbet).** Watercolor on ivory, 4 1/2″ x 3 3/4″ (11.4 x 9.5 cm) framed. Massachusetts, inscribed on back of frame "Elizabeth Freeman / Mumbet / Susan Sedgewick / Fecit 1811 / E. M. B. Sedgwick / 1868 /." Courtesy the Massachusetts Historical Society, Boston. (1)

261. Anonymous. **Bracelet.** Gold metal, 1/4″ x 2 1/4″ (.6 x 5.7 cm) in diameter. Engraved on clasp "Mumbet." America, c. 1800-1810. Courtesy Massachusetts Historical Society, Boston. (1)

262. John Habersham (Collector of the Customs for Savannah, Georgia), **Report to Oliver Wolcott, (Secretary of the Treasury) denying the claim for damages submitted by Elizabeth Massey.** Autograph manuscript copy, 10″ x 8″ (25.4 x 20.3 cm). Savannah [Georgia], December 16, 1797. National Archives, Washington, D.C. (6)

263. Anonymous. **On BRYAN SHEENEN...** Broadside, 15 5/16″ x 10 5/32″ (38.9 x 25.8 cm). [Salem, Massachusetts], January 16, 1772. Courtesy Massachusetts Historical Society, Boston. (1)

264. Anonymous. **An Account of the Life of Bryan Sheehen.** Broadside, 15 1/4″ x 10 1/8″ (38.8 x 25.7 cm). Portsmouth [N.H.?], January 16, 1772. Historical Society of Pennsylvania, Philadelphia. (2-6)

265. John W. Kirn. **A Genuine Sketch of the Trial of Mary Cole for the Wilful Murder of Her Mother, Agnes Thuers.** Printed pamphlet, 8 3/8″ x 5 1/8″ (21.2 x 13 cm). New Jersey, 1812. American Antiquarian Society, Worcester, Mass. (1)